SUCCESS SUTRA

SUCCESS IS NOT A SALAD,
IT IS A WHOLE MEAL

SUCCESS SUTRA

Aruna Jethwani

Sterling Paperbacks

STERLING PAPERBACKS
An imprint of
Sterling Publishers (P) Ltd.
A-59, Okhla Industrial Area, Phase-II,
New Delhi-110020.
Tel: 26387070, 26386209; Fax: 91-11-26383788
E-mail: mail@sterlingpublishers.com
www.sterlingpublishers.com

Success Sutra
© 2010, Aruna Jethwani
ISBN 978 81 207 4918 4

All rights are reserved.
No part of this publication may be reproduced, stored in a retrieval system or transmitted, in any form or by any means, mechanical, photocopying, recording or otherwise, without prior written permission of the original publisher.

Printed in India

Printed and Published by Sterling Publishers Pvt. Ltd.,
New Delhi-110 020.

Acknowledgements

I take this opportunity to express my sincere gratitude to Dr. Arjun Batra for his valuable guidance. I owe gratitude to Prof. Uma Shashi Bhalerao for her practical suggestions. My friend Beena Rajeev Menon, has been kind enough to type the manuscript. I thank her from the bottom of my heart.

I owe special gratitude to Shri S K Ghai, CMD, Sterling Publishers, for readily accepting the manuscript. His team has worked hard to bring the book to its present form. My heartfelt thanks to them.

Preface

To begin with, success is like happiness. Everyone wants it. Whatever the perception of success—an apex position in professional life, a healthy social life, a loving and lasting relationship, or just being a good human being, the goal is to achieve it, live it and enjoy it.

So fix a goal, be motivated, seek a route to it, and achieve it. The world is changing very fast. In the changing world and the changing environment, the goals too have to change, and the road to success is no longer a given formula that you can apply irrespective of your situation in life.

The very perception of success is changing, success is no longer a single achievement, it is multidimensional. It is a balance of various goals which make life meaningful and fulfilling. It is this 'balance' that this book will help you to discover.

Success is holistic. Aim at the whole.
And you will be happy.

Albert Einstein's Formula for Success

A (Success) = x (Work) + y (Play) + z (Keep mouth shut)

This common formula, is the famous 'Mantra' for success. However, recent studies by well known philosophers like Malcolm Gladwell, has revealed the inadequacy of the formula. According to them, 'Hard work + Luck + Talent' are not sufficient for success. Some add emotional quotient, and spiritual quotient to the much accepted formula. However, recent scientific discoveries show that besides talent, luck, hard work, passion and positivism, there are other elements such as family values, social background and cultural traits which account for success.

The following pages provide the road map for holistic and wholesome success.

Contents

Acknowledgements	v
Preface	vii
Introduction	xi

SELF MANAGEMENT

The Art of Living with Oneself	3
Managing the Mind	6
Coping Strategies	15
Mind Therapies	43
Managing the Body	51

MANAGING RELATIONSHIPS

How to Build Good Relationships	61

SUCCESS WITH CAREER

For a Successful Career...	79
Old Wine Of Success	86
There is Always a Solution	93

Leadership Secrets	98
Success Through The Power Within	105
Guidelines for Success	109
The Inner Scape	112
Disappointed? Bounce Back	116

THE SECRET ROUTE

Discovering the Route	125

Introduction

We all aspire for success in life. In the world we live in, 'failure' is an obnoxious term, yet, very few of us understand what success really means.

To some, success is being at the top of the career chart, to some others it means wealth and affluence. To some it is synonymous with money, to the others it is some kind of emotional fulfillment. Perhaps, success involves a bit of everything.

What is Success?

A human being is a multidimensional dynamo. He has many sides to his personality. Success in a single area does not give him the satisfaction which his personality needs. In present times, the heady feeling of success which comes from riding high on the galloping horse of money is just not enough. It leaves a vacuum in other areas of life. As the saying goes, man does not live by bread alone. He has other needs too.

Hence we say, Success is Holistic!

- Success is not wealth or affluence.
- Success is not Status, Power and Leadership.
- Success is not Popularity.
- Success is not being in the driver's seat.
- Success is not the apex authority.

One definition of success which I like is the one given by Swami Chinmayanand.

"A successful man is one who can lay a firm foundation with the bricks others throw at him". Swami Chinmayanand's concept implies the following pragmatism:

- Make every misfortune a fortune.
- Do not lick your wounds but, face the brickbats with courage, turning them into the strength of a character.
- Do not return an eye for an eye and a tooth for a tooth.

As Mahatma Gandhi said, that would leave the world with blind people.

There are many parts to our living. But the three areas of our life most important to us are:

- Our inner and outer selves,
- Our relationships, personal and social
- Our education, career and profession

Maybe we do not view their significance in that order. To some of us, our personal relationships are more important and meaningful than our careers; to others, profession outweighs all considerations and to yet others, it is 'oneself' that is the most valuable channel to switch on.

Simply stated, success is holistic. It cannot be divided into parts. The above three areas are equally important. A certain connectivity links them, and it shall be our endeavour to integrate them into panoramic 'movie' called life, the beautiful.

Let's therefore come down to brass-tacks. We need the tools and a technique for the holistic success. The best tool is management. We can identify three areas of management.

- Self-management
- Relationships Management
- Education and Career Management

Self-management will guide us on how to integrate our various 'selves' in order to overcome the many problems of life arising from 'self–multiplicity'. It will also guide us how to tackle problems of life like loneliness, frustration, depression, failure and anxiety. But the scope of self-management is not just that. It is much wider.

Self-management will teach us how to relate to our own self, and of course give us tools and techniques for transforming our Negativism into Positivism. It will help us link with ourselves, and that way turn our wishes into horses which we will ride successfully.

Relationship management is an area we all are aware of. The day we are born, we are part of a family, a society, a nation. In fact we begin our first relationship in the womb—our relationship with our mother. Relationship management is a tricky area, because that is the area of 'emotions and enigmas.' It is the area of management which requires the skills, which are to be cultivated in order to be successful. It needs therapies and all kinds of inputs to make it successful.

Education and Career Management can be put into software, once your hard disks of 'self' and 'relationship' are ready. The software for success in Career Windows 2009 gives us various options. Either we go back in history and dig out Vedas, Vedanta, Kalidas, and *Bhagwad Gita* and apply the time tested values and ethics to our self or we can also look into future and anticipate changes and be prepared for them.

Success Has a Beautiful Face
And it is a bright and expensive face. This face is the result of certain innate qualities; one of it is looking at the brighter side of things. I have for my neighbour, a highly successful person. On New Year's Eve, I wanted to send him a cake. Out of curiosity a naughty child opened the box and put his finger into it.

"You cannot send that cake to him,' yelled my daughter. I could not waste the cake. I cut it into half and sent him the untouched half cake. The family was angry with me but not the recipient. He thanked me profusely. When I apologized for sending only a half cake, he said, "When people send a cake all dressed up, it is often more out of demonstration. Sending half a cake is rare, for it comes with love from the bottom of your heart you shared your cake. And sharing is invaluable."

Success has a soft face and a tough mind.

Success Has a Beautiful Mind

There is a famous story of the great scientist, Thomas Edison. After putting in thirty year's labour, he did not despair. He did not cry over split milk. He began planning his research all over again. Thomas Edison had a tough mind, which could withstand the immense loss of his research papers. Thomas Edison had courage, will power, and positive attitude. All put together he gave the world a rare gift; that of electricity. It is a great boon for the progress of mankind. With a little training of the mind, we can develop will power, courage and positive attitude. A wild horse can be trained, why not the human mind?

Success Has a Soul

Success comes out of inner strength. The inner strength comes from one's Higher self. Every human being has a potential within; for in every man is the *Atman*, the Infinite power. It is a limitless *shakti*. Once awakened, it can help one scale great heights. It can help one touch the sky and fulfil all one's dreams.

A man of inner strength has courage to face difficulties, surmount obstacles and cross hurdles.

How to build inner strength? You may well ask how to build faith? You may build faith through meditation, through reading inspirational literature or through spiritual guidance. Inner strength comes out of deep spirituality. Inner strength makes a person firm, decisive, confident, and self reliant. All that you have to do is to become aware of the great power within you. The awareness itself will make you strong and prepare you for positive results.

SELF MANAGEMENT

The Art of Living with Oneself

Here are a few tips on the art of living with oneself:

Acceptance Of Self

For years I used to feel guilty for drinking cups of tea, till I met a woman who was proud of being a tea drinker. "Hey, tea is my companion, my stimulator, I need it. Be ashamed of it? Not at all! I am proud that I don't drink alcohol. I enjoy the light flavoured Assamese tea! What's wrong with it?"

True. There is nothing wrong with this harmless luxury. We should accept all our weaknesses as a part of our personality. That does not mean that we remain latched on to our bad habits or 'immoral' traits. But given the reasonable latitude and the acceptable paradigms, if there are a few not so good habits or a few flaws, it should not matter to us. Even the moon has flaws, as the saying goes.

How do we learn the art of accepting ourselves as we are?

Physical Acceptance: Look into the mirror and accept your face, physical features and body. Accept it as a gift of God, which is to be kept pure, clean and shining. Find beauty in it. Believe me. Everybody is beautiful or can be made to look beautiful. Repeat to yourself the mantra, "I accept myself as a gratitude to God!" Let's go a step further. "Love thyself! Learn to love yourself as you are." Forget the minor flaws and think 'beautiful'.

Stay Awake. Stay Alive.

After you have accepted yourself, learn to enjoy the small pleasures of life. Stay awake. Take interest in your hobbies and expand the horizon of your experiences. Move on to a richer and fuller life. The Vedic chant *"Uttishthat Jagrat!"* (Awake, Arise!) can be read both spiritually and inspirationally.

A Palm Tree Always Dances

Rigidity is one of the causes of breakdown. A rigid mindset can bring in all the malaise of the fallout effects of change. During a storm a palm tree swings and sways, to survive; but a stiff tree is uprooted, and a stiff branch is broken. Be like a palm tree, learn to be flexible.

Ownership Of Self Is An Asset

It is the poverty of thought which makes us lose sight of the greatest asset man possesses—himself—body, mind and soul. Ownership of this great machine of live ingredients (*panch tatva*, water, air, ether, earth and fire) i.e. ourselves is the most precious asset – and we should rejoice in its being.

The Self Balance Sheet

Evaluate the worth of this great asset. Have your balance sheet of strengths and weaknesses right. If the balance sheet is positive, you are already a bird of freedom. If it is negative, you have to mark the year, to cover up the losses. Is your weakness; lack of communication, lack of 'give in', lack of moral strength, lack of sincerity? Once you identify the 'weakness', it is easy to cure it.

Be A Bird In The Sky

The relationship with the Self should be such that you should be in a position to take off any time you feel like. In other words, some amount of detachment in your day to day work is necessary. Work honestly, perform your duties with love and care, but not with attachment, not with expectations. Be free from the strings of attachment or expectation. Be a bird in the sky.

Linkage With Self

Acceptance of self is easy. It is difficult to link ourselves with the inner self. There are three ways of forging this wonderful link. The link which brings peace and harmony.

Practical Exercise

Whatever your lifestyle, you can always incorporate a simple exercise in it.

It is a simple breathing exercise and a sure way to link you to yourself. Sit in a silent corner, and as you breathe, say,

> I breathe in love, breathe out bitterness
> I breathe in abundance, breathe out lack
> I breathe in harmony, breathe out discord
> I breathe in health, breathe out sickness
> I breathe in joy, breathe out sorrow
> I breathe in freedom, breathe out bondage
> I breathe in wisdom, breathe out ignorance.

This exercise will refresh your body, mind and soul.

Man has a mind and a heart, and the two are opposite to each other. Mind is rational and restless. Heart is emotional and also restless. We have to learn to manage both.

Managing the Mind

What Is Mind?
"Mind is the seat of impulses and feelings and it is common to all living creatures." The human mind works deeper and in more complex ways because it has intellect. The mind is also defined as a flow of thought just as a river is a flow of water.

The mind has three layers of consciousness; the conscious, the unconscious and the subconscious. The Conscious mind is the one you are aware of; the one with which you reason, the one with which you discern. The unconscious mind is the 'natural' mind, by virtue of condition/habit. The subtle mind of course is the subconscious which is very powerful and the maker of your Destiny.

Mind; The Primal Energy
Energy follows thoughts. We may by the power of thought change our very circumstances and conditions. All that is about us and around us is but the expression of thought. All that we see built by the hand of man was once merely a thought in the mind of man.

Likewise, Nature is the expression of the thought of God. That thought might have had its source in the energy of 'will' of God, but it is the thought that has 'realised' or 'actualised' the will. By the potency of thought you may

Managing the Mind

acquire wealth and power and the things of your heart's desire.

We may draw a simile between 'the thought' and 'electricity'. Electricity is latent in the atmosphere, but serves no recognized purpose until it is conserved and gathered up. We see it in the lightning during a thunderstorm or in the friction between bamboo trees caught in frenetic wind. We know then, that electricity can be used in a thousand and one ways. So the thought is planted in the mind, germinates and ultimately finds expression in action.

Man must realize that the circumstance of today is largely the outcome of his thoughts in the past, and in no small measure determines his circumstances of tomorrow. War, peace, prosperity and progress are all man's creation by his thought. He also, in no small measure determines his circumstance of tomorrow.

Mind is not mere grey cells, or the brain. Mind has thoughts, which are 'subtle' energy/force.

On an average, a human being has 52,000 thoughts in a day. The thoughts may be divided into four categories:
- Positive thoughts
- Negative thoughts
- Strong thoughts
- Weak thoughts

Thoughts are 'energy'. Therefore, they have the ability to 'materialize'. Hence positive thoughts, if strong, are converted into 'actuality'. Weak thoughts, passing thoughts, fleeting thoughts, thoughts of the past are a drain on mental energy.

Thoughts of the future, are a cause of worry and drain energy. Save mental energy, avoid wastage of thought energy. One can avoid wasting mental energy by keeping thoughts under control. It is said that the mind is like a wild horse and it should be trained and controlled as one. In the movie *Wild Horse*, the horse is trained by the trainer, by the 'Carrot and Stick' method, i.e., reward for improvement and flogging for failing to obey. Perhaps, we too can practice this method and train the mind to be in its own place. After training the mind to be in its rightful place, we can control it and command it. But it is not an easy job.

In the *Bhagwad Gita*, Arjuna tells Lord Krishna that the control of the mind is more difficult than controlling the wind. The mind has often been compared to an unbridled horse which romps around wildly.

Swami Vivekananda has said that the mind is like an intoxicated monkey jumping from one branch of a tree to another. The mind is also compared to a river, which is a collection of drops of water—the drops of water being the *sanskars* of previous births.

The mind is also compared to a disturbed pond containing many impurities, and one has to stop the flow of impurities.

Managing the Mind

> *The King, the beggar, and the saint*
> *All are disconsolate;*
> *Only he who controls his mind*
> *Is happy and content.*
>
> *Thy mind goes far away*
> *To all that occurred in the past,*
> *And will occur in future,*
> *Call it back to thyself*
> *So that it may remain*
> *Under thy control*
>
> **Kabir**

This provides the clue to how to control the mind.

When thoughts run helter-skelter, bring them to the 'Present'; this is called the power of the Now. Once concentrated, the mind can achieve the impossible. That is why it is said "A Man is what he thinks".

The mind with its emotional and psychological pressures is known to have an effect on the well-being of human health. Negative emotions like anger, irritation, frustration, fear, anxiety, worry and loneliness can cause illness; physical and mental. Thus the body–mind coordination and soul, that divine light inside a human being, also have effect on a person's well-being. For example, people of prayer and faith always glow with positivism. They are calm and composed and healthy vibrations emanate from them. To some extent meditation and mantra help both mind and soul (Soul, like the mind is also energy.)

How to Get Rid of Negative Thoughts

For a long time, I suffered from Negative thoughts. I overcome 'Negativism' through 'retracing the emotion'. My negative thoughts took the form of 'Fear of accidents'. I would step out of the house and I would panic at the sight of chaotic traffic. Every time panic gripped me, I replaced the negative picture with the positive one. Like the fear of vehicle accident was replaced by imagining myself driving joyfully. Immediately the 'panic' and the 'throbbing' of heart would stop and I would feel relaxed.

'Retracing emotions' is a Buddhist technique. Just the other day, the Dalai Lama visited our campus. My niece Urmilla was with me. She and another woman bowed to his Holiness. At that moment His Holiness the Dalai Lama was busy talking to a monk and then moved on. What was the reaction of Urmilla and the other woman?

Urmilla was all excitement, she was overwhelmed and she exclaimed, "How fortunate I'm to have *'Darshan'* of Dalai Lama and seek his blessings."

The other woman's face fell. She frowned visibly. She was thoroughly disappointed and said, "The Dalai Lama did not even look at me. I have come all the way from Kolhapur to get his blessings. My efforts are wasted."

The same situation engendered two different reactions.

Exercise

- You can control the mind and learn to concentrate through *Khetchri Mudra*.
- One important *Mudra*, which links physical body to mind, is *Khetchri Mudra*. The word *Khetchri* is derived from '*Kha* – bird' '*cha*'– *charatti*, i.e. moves. The mind can also move without limitations of time and space. Yogis under strict guidance practiced this. Today laymen can take advantage of this concept of freedom.
- Meditate
- Sit in silence, every few hours
- Pull your mind to 'now' whenever it strays from attention

The Power of Imagination – Day Dreaming

As children we are often reprimanded, 'Hey, you big dreamer,' or 'you silly child, stop day dreaming,' and this piece of cake (advice) is 'iced' by narrating the famous story of Sheikh Chillie – who dreamt a bit too much and met with disaster. But his dismal fate was the result of unscientific dreaming.

Day Dreaming is the science of imagination. "Day Dreaming" says Nikhet, the HRD Guru, "performs a multifarious role. It gives freedom to the mind which eases it out of anxiety. In the process, it also expresses its natural self and latent needs. It creates images which find expression in reality."

There are umpteen people who lived in poverty but day dreamed of great things. The Lord Mayor of London is a leaf from history to vouch for this fact. Indian filmstar Anil Kapoor used to live in a *chawl* and dreamt of becoming a superstar. His dreams came true albeit, with hard work. It is said that Man can create anything he can imagine. Indeed his mental images manufacture the conditions and experiences of his life and affairs. Man's only limitation lies in the limited use he makes of his imagination.

Our sages had understood the nature of the mind just as Karl Jung had. The conscious mind thinks, the subconscious mind accepts and obeys it. Our thoughts seep into the subconscious mind and begin to work. Very often the subconscious mind is compared to a fertile soil. The soil simply receives whatever the farmer chooses to sow and thus it produces what has been sowed into it.

Hypnosis therapy uses the subconscious mind to work into actual experiences. In a state of hypnosis the subconscious mind is given the command to 'Be a leader', 'Be successful', 'Be a great name' and the subconscious mind carries out the orders. It is this mind which receives commands from the universe – sixth sense or what we call paranormal phenomenon. Nothing is impossible for the imagination. True, sometimes it takes longer for our mental images to produce results, the more we hold on to our images the finer our results.

Says a regular practitioner of 'Mental Images', "If I get a feeling of peace, I know the results will be quick, if not, then I have to work hard to get the desired results. I then seek the help of God almighty."

The imaging power of the mind is fascinating, the more one develops it, the better one feels. At times we are assailed by doubts and therefore we face difficulty in developing this powerful tool.

Thus, what we dream of, or imagine is received by the subconscious mind; which obeys it.

Imaging/Creative Visualisation

A twentieth century philosopher has said, "The imagination is a wonderful creative power. It builds all things out of the substance. When you associate it with faith, you make things just as real as those which God makes, for man is a co-creator with God. Whatever you form in the mind and have faith in, will become substantial."

Creative Visualisation too is based on the above principle. As Shakti Gawain, the author of *Creative Visualisation* says, 'Creative Visualisation is the technique of using your imagination to create what you want in your life.' Prayer and Mantras work on a similar principle, i.e., suggestion to the subconscious mind. Here are some practical suggestions:

- Imagine success, victory, happiness, or your heart's desire
- Clear your mind of negative thoughts
- Pray and have faith in the universe
- Reaffirm your thoughts, images

- Believe in yourself and your ability
- Believe that the Cosmic Power/God is cooperating with you

It is probable that your image may change, your inner urges may surface and take on the shape of new images. Your own conscious thinking may change. The images which are more powerful will be realized. Sometimes the time element in the functioning of the natural laws may be long, at other times it may be short or even instantaneous. Time Spirit is also a natural law. People who have clarity of thought and purity of mind can achieve their heart's desire by merely thinking of it consciously. Their mental energy is powerful enough for 'actualization'.

Certainly, the power of imagination may not work. If we are tension ridden, the tension creates unnatural or imperfect images.

Finally, believe that God wants you to have more than what you already have because God is the Main Giver. To end with a quotation on God's image of success – "The Divine image of success now manifests for me. Then let it work, don't limit yourself by becoming upset, or disappointed if your success comes in unforeseen or in completely different ways. God's image of success for you is complete and satisfying."

Exercise: Do *Kapalbhati*, a yoga *asan* that gives clarity to the mind. Then relax and imagine success and the ways to achieve it step by step.

"Behaviour is an important tool for success. Behave clearly, gently, amply, kindly, friendly, cheerfully and boldly."

Most of us swing between 'highs' and 'lows'. Sometimes the cool breeze that touches us is like a balm. Sometimes the very same breeze irritates us. The breeze is the same, nevertheless, we react differently. Why? Our mental state keeps changing. Our mental state is the result of many forces that can be managed and controlled.

Among the common 'moods' which need to be managed are depression, loneliness, and boredom. All these moods are interactive and cumulative in their effect.

We will deal with these 'four' moods later in this book.

Coping Strategies

Coping With Boredom

The Vedas say, "*Do not lead a dull dead life. Live a life of zest and enthusiasm.*" The *Atharvaveda* states, "*Live a life of living man. Die not, live with the spirit of elevated souls.*"

Boredom is an urban disease of the 20th and 21st century. This new malaise strikes a child of three as well as a man of eighty. In spite of the variety of entertainment available (radio, television, movies and now video games and internet chat) man finds himself at a loose end. Haven't we heard the common phrases, 'Life is boring', or 'I'm bored to death'?

What leads to boredom?

Surface Living

Osho has explained this in a beautiful verse called the 'first layer of personality.'

> *Social formality has become a frozen thing with millions of people they live on this layer,*
>
> *They never move beyond it, etiquette, mannerism, words, and chatter – always on the surface.*
>
> *They talk, not to communicate,*
> *They talk to avoid communication.*
> *They talk to avoid embarrassing situations.*
> *In which they encounter the other.*
> *They are 'closed' people.*
> *In fact they are dead people.*

Osho himself has given the reason why people are dead –

> *An unhealthy person,*
> *Smiles – does not mean it,*
> *Laughs – does not mean it,*
> *He never means anything,*
> *His whole life is just an exhibition.*
> *He cannot enjoy it, because he*
> *Cannot move within words.*

He means, do not pretend. Do not be superficial. Be creative, be your own self.

Lack of sufficient activity

There is a lack of balance in our activities. The new syndrome of being 'focused' and 'single-minded' pulls us away from our hobbies or the activities, which we enjoy. For instance, if we love to have our friends at home, the long hours at work prevent us from doing so and we feel restless and bored. If we love theatre, we find neither the time nor the energy to participate.

Our livelihood has become very important; it is a matter of survival in these days of cut-throat competition. The modern trend of 'work hard and party harder' is again imbalanced; because 'enjoy hard' tends to be very formalized like discos, hi-fi parties, late nights etc. which bring temporary excitement, but leave one feeling dull and bored the next morning.

Inability to enjoy simple pleasures of life

Do you enjoy arranging flowers in a vase? Or collecting shells on a sea beach? Or baking a cake for a dear one? Or having an ice cream and sipping tea by the river side? Do you love to run with the children and laugh with them? If not then you have lost the 'wonder' in life. That feeling of excitement which makes life tick.

Doing things which are not to your liking?
Each one of us is made of a different mould. Every personality has likes and dislikes. If a student does not like mathematics and is compelled, by circumstances, to major in it, he is bound to be bored by the 'drama of maths'. Similarly, if a science student who loves laboratory experiments is made to study and recite poetry, he may find it very unpleasant or irrelevant. We all know from experience that the work we enjoy is a pleasure, but the work we dislike is a headache.

Narrow human relationships
All of us grow up with different attitudes towards human relationships. Some like to limit their relationships to their 'first blood relations' or to 'their few friends'; yet others to 'wife/husband and children'. Somewhere in life, these relationships tend to become 'weak', 'vague', 'lacking communication' either due to distance or time constraints and then we are left high and dry. Being a loner is one thing, being isolated is another.

Seven simple solutions to beat boredom
Continuous excitement or perpetual activities are certainly not the answer. One has to go deeper to rid oneself of the disease.

Be involved in whatever you are doing
Even a simple greeting like "Hello, how are you?" should be meaningful. It should not be a mere etiquette. It should be a feeling straight from the heart. You will see the warmth of the response. For it is a greeting from man to man and not from one robot to another.

Enjoy doing whatever you are doing
It may be a simple chore of making a cup of coffee or a tedious job of cleaning vegetables or cupboards. Think of the end product, not of the means. The lovely meals and the well arranged clothes. Cleaning cupboards is a psychological act. By throwing away the unwanted things you throw clutter out of your mind. The physical act becomes a mental act.

Look for variety in life
Break the monotony of living with 'surprise' visits, get together for prayer meet or *bhajan* sessions in the house. Alternatively change your schedule. Watch different types of TV programmes. Sometimes change over to radio for live programmes.

According to Swami Harshananda, one should also try to develop a sense of art-appreciation, and develop the capacity to enjoy good music, dance performance, theatre or painting. Which means, do not merely listen, watch or view, but enjoy, appreciate, participate, sympathise, empathise to feel the thrill of it.

Expand your interacting group
Online chat or jokes are fine but these merely help pass the time but do not meet your need for interaction. However small your group, you can always deepen your involvement.

You may also work out greater association by offering a helping hand to various organizations around. Someone said to me the other day, "In old age, be like a river which has collected many tributaries to form a voluminous flow of water. Do not thin out with the years, widen out".

Look for excitement in everyday living
Rearrange your furniture. Bring in a bit of nature, especially flowers, as flowers have the power to soothe and healing

properties. Just imagine it was merely a fall of an apple that led Newton to discover the Law of Gravitation. It was the sight of a mere stone, which led Michelangelo to sculpt the most beautiful 'Man' in the world. It was watching sunrays on water that made Vincent Van Gogh go in for those bright yellow strokes.

Pick up an unusual hobby
It may be as expensive as collecting cinema wardrobes or as cheap as collecting straw hats or straw folk fans or even stones from riverbeds or shells from the beach or flower petals from a garden. Collect them and use them. I collect moss only to return it to plants. But the thrill of searching and finding moss is exciting!

Find new routes – free from moribund mind
Discover new picnic spots, new mountain treks, new nature 'holes', new eating joints, new friends, new movies, new music, new *Ramayana*, new *Mahabharata*, new books and new stories. I am sure there are a lot of untold stories waiting for you.

Coping With Loneliness
Loneliness comes in various moods and forms, in fact, in as many shades and colours as life itself. Loneliness may be of mind, heart or spirit. Nevertheless, it is loneliness. Some of the causes of loneliness are:
- Break up of a relationship
- Family strife
- Relocation of job, house, town or city
- Personal loss of a friend or relative
- Retirement from a job/employment
- Ill health and physical immobility

- Alienation i.e., separation from social, physical, psychological and spiritual forces of life

Whatever the cause, loneliness can be overcome with a little effort and willingness to change. There are three relationships, which form the core of living. The first is with the society in which you live. This relationship is of the 'blood' that is family, and extends to neighbourhood, community and nation at large. Social networking and social connectivity can strengthen this relationship. Family hug, holidays for bonding and community service are the bonding techniques that are gaining ground now.

The second relationship is with the self. We live in this world not as one individual but as two—the inner self and the outer self. The two selves should be integrated through yoga, prayer, meditation and reading good literature.

The third is the relationship with Nature or the Universe. Develop an exciting relationship with nature. Remember, it has been created for you. You are a part, though a miniscule one, of the great scheme of creation, so you cannot be separate from it.

Any relationship is a matter of the input – output ratio. One should continuously pour inputs into life to make it full.

Seven simple practical suggestions to beat loneliness:

- Join a voluntary organization, like Rotary Club, Lions Club, neighbourhood support groups such as Keep Your City Clean, Senior Citizens Club and Youth Club, and help social channels operating in your city.
- Adopt a tree or a plant. Talk to it if you please. Feel the thrill of its response. Grow plants and make them a part of your family. Love animals and bring them home into your lives. Pets are good company.
- Grow social. Note down birthdays and anniversaries. Use them as channels of communication. I recently visited an

old man who noted down my address. When I remarked that he would never visit my home, he smiled, "This is to send you a Diwali card."
- Create space and beauty around you. Rearrange your furniture whenever possible. It breaks the monotony of life. Fill the space with beauty. Do not throw away empty bottles, but fill them with cuttings of money plant or wild creepers. Place them together and soon you will have a green garden inside your home.
- Take up an absorbing hobby; crosswords, card playing, scrabble, collecting items, painting, singing, clay modelling are some of them. Join relevant clubs for inspiration and activity.
- Make use of cinema therapy. Watch a comedy or light-hearted movie when feeling lonely and low.
- Join a meditation group or *Satsang* or *Gita* classes or yoga, *Vedanta* study classes. Be a member of movements such as The Art of Living, The Humanistic Movement or Sathya Sai Seva Samiti. There are an endless number of such organizations and fellowship groups, all waiting to embrace you in their fold.

Lonely? Loneliness will vanish the moment you are bonded, linked, hooked, and aligned. Try it .

Coping With Depression

Down in the dumps? Irritated? Caught up in a tunnel? The dark web of negativism is not easy to break. Surely, there is a way out. First, let us identify the cause.
- Depression can be physiological such as after menopause or caused by chemical deficiency.
- It can be the result of an unhealthy emotional life i.e., emotional starvation such as lack of love, lack of a sense of belonging, or failure of a primary personal relationship etc.

- Depression can be physiological. A rigid mindset which cannot accept changes, situations or traumas. A highly sensitive personality swings up with joy and comes down with a thud at the slightest provocation.
- Depression is a cocoon hard to break. It is a rock bottom from where it is difficult to come out without outside help. The outside help can be found in a friend, a spiritual guide, a holy man, a psychologist, or in the family. You need a shoulder to cry on; someone to share a burden with; a ventilator to let the fresh air in.

Seven simple ways to overcome Depression

There are several therapies for treating depression. Anti-depressant pills, *Pranic* healing, laughing therapy, and cinema therapy. My seven simple ways are as effective as any therapy. They are:

Surya Shakti

Avail of the great solar energy. It is our ancient tradition to bow down to the sun and seek its 'blessings'. In today's jargon it would mean to 'empower oneself with sun-energy.' This is how you go about it. First thing in the morning, after your bath, 'take in the pure rays of the rising sun.' Do not look directly at the sun. Pour water, and through the 'pouring water, take in the light of the sunrays. This simple act increases your level of energy and empowers you with brightness.

Activity is the key solution

Depression can be offset by constructive activity. Work has a great healing quality. It absorbs you; your thinking is tied to a particular 'pillar'. It hooks the mind. Plan your day; fill it with activity, leaving only minimum time for sleep and leisure.

Be your own Mirror

> Up the bay my ships will sail –
> So I never quite despair
> Nor let my courage fail;
> And some day when skies are fair.
>
> **Robert Barry Coffin**

Talk to yourself, and ask the reason why you are down in the dumps. Is it frustration? Is it despair? Is it unacceptability? Is it some blankness or vacuum in your life? Is it loss of a job, or a friend or beloved one?

Once the cause is known perhaps a solution may be found. Self-dialogue may clear off cobwebs and nameless fears of insecurity. Insecurity, the feeling of being unwanted, futility of activity, or fatalistic attitude may drop you into a pit. But one has to make an effort to climb out of it. One has to stand outside of oneself, to see oneself in the mirror. The image itself may offer a solution. Beautify the ugly image in the mirror. Use both the cosmic and cosmetic aids. The cosmic aids are prayer, meditation, and music.

Do something for somebody

An old woman lived alone down the street. She spent long empty hours, no, not whining or complaining, but crocheting baby frocks, baking birthday cakes, embroidering napkins and handkerchiefs, all of which were gifted during Christmas, on birthdays and as thank you gifts to visitors. The whole neighbourhood loved her. Her relatives looked forward to her cakes and cookies. This woman used her 'terminal time' usefully, spreading cheer and happiness.

A widow once complained, "It is fine for you people to say to help others.

What if I need help myself? What if I do not have the money to visit hospitals or orphanages?" No problem. Gift a smile. It costs nothing. And there are umpteen people around us who need this bit of cheer, this bit of a smile.

Count your blessings

This may sound clichéd, but unless we count our blessings we cannot turn ourselves to positive thinking. Take a piece of paper and jot down the 'good' things you have in life, and against it note down the things you lack, or desire.

It helps a bit to remind ourselves of the ditty,

"I had no shoes and I complained, until I met a person who had no feet."

There is this famous story of a rich man. He had a daughter who desired to marry a young man, of modest means. "Tell the young man to make a fortune, before he comes to ask for your hand," the stern father told his daughter. The daughter came back after a few days with a note from the young man. It read 'I have two millions.' When the father met the young man, he casually enquired about his wealth. The young man said, "I have two precious assets which are worth two millions." "Which are these assets?" the girl's father asked anxiously. "They are my two eyes."

The girl's father was aghast with anger. "How can you call them two millions?"

"Perhaps more," replied the young man ,

"Would you exchange your eyes for two millions?"

"Never," replied the father. "Exactly so, I have healthy eyes, healthy lungs, healthy brain. I have all these assets which are worth billions of rupees."

True. You are an asset for yourself. Your very being on this beautiful planet is a celebration. You have to realize it.

Get into this main stream of life

Just do not sit and brood. Inertia adds to the depression. Move. Go and jog and meet people on the way. Visit a library and make friends. Join a community program. Run if you must, to shake off that lethargy. Find 'connectivity' somewhere. Depression comes out of melancholy and isolation. Be a church member, or hop onto a kitty bandwagon. The bottom line is, "Mingle, mingle, do not remain single!"

Try out yoga

According to Dr Sandhya Pitke who teaches Yoga, "Depression is the result of one's management of inferior or superior expression of one's ego." She recommends the practice of *Ishwar Pranidhana*, which means surrendering to the Supreme Energy source. Faith in the Supreme Being eliminates paranoid ego.

Feel Nature's presence

He is everywhere. It is when we turn away our face from the Great Cosmic energy that we feel the darkness and we see the shadows.

I read a beautiful story of a young girl who complained to her mother, of shadows in front of her whenever she walked. The mother quietly replied, "You see the shadow in front of you because the sun is behind you. What you see is your own shadow. Turn your face to the sun and the shadow will vanish." True, most of our dark frightening shadows are the result of an existence with our back to the Great Energy – The Eternal Energy of Nature.

Coping with Fear

We are born with fear, and we live and die with fear. There are a thousand and one fears. Fear of accidents, failure, success, ill health, rejection, losing a dear one, death, heights, 'locations', sorrow and blankness and fear of the known and unknown. Fear of any kind numbs the mind, freezes the brain, stuns the body, holds up blood circulation, increases heart beat and palpitation. Fear causes phobias, mental imbalance and irresponsible behaviour.

Our ancient Vedas, tell human beings, to be fearless

> O resplendent God Almighty,
> May we live without fear
> In thy friendship,
> invincible and unconquered Lord,
> We offer our eulogy unto thee.
> **Samveda 828**

Fear is a poison that quickly circulates through the entire system, paralyzing the will. Fear is a merciless Master. Strike fear with the weapon of the spirit—the word of God! But faith is a difficult thing. To hitch oneself to the unknown and to relax is difficult to achieve.

How can you be free from fear?

- Psychologists will advice – Desensitize to the external stimuli.
- The holy ones will ask you to light a candle and recite a mantra, a hymn, or sit down in meditation and surrender all to God.
- Yet others will advise—Be friendly with the thing you fear the most. Familiarity breeds fearlessness.
- Follow the Buddha – retrace your 'fear thoughts', to negate their effect. If you fear a fall, reverse it. Imagine you have risen without hurting yourself.
- The best antidote to fear is Love. Between love and love, there is no place for fear. Love is positive and fear negative. If you are afraid of going up on the stage and delivering a speech, the simplest way to overcome it would be to send out loving vibrations to the audience.

Coping Strategies

You can practice the following mental exercises to overcome the fear of masses. This fear stems from self-doubt.

Before going to the stage you can recite,

- Well, I am one of you, I love you. If I make a mistake, do forgive me.
- Love the subject of your talk. "This is what I love; this is what I want to share with the world."
- Visualise yourself as a friendly speaker, delivering the message in a most relaxed manner
- Provide yourself with some physical aids, like deep breathing, harnessing energy through loosening of your body and drinking half a glass of water thereafter
- Take the support of your god, Guru or Deity and offer a small prayer, seeking his/her help. Ask the higher forces to cooperate with you
- Reaffirm to yourself that you will do it successfully
- Chant a mantra or sing a hymn for that mental strength
- Wear your success 'Charm' or 'Talisman' for that 'emotional faith'

Of course there are as many ways to overcome fear as there are fears.

Eleanor Roosevelt has written:

> You gain strength,
> Courage and confidence
> By every experience in which
> You really stop
> To look Fear in the face.
> You are able to say to yourself
> "I lived through this horror
> I can take the next thing that comes along."
> ....you must do the things you
> Think you cannot do.

Accept the challenge. Here are a few names of women from Pune who overcame their fears by accepting the challenge:

> *Bharati Dhotare was always terrified of water, learnt swimming with determination and with will power she made it to the finishing line.*
>
> *Sometimes the 'fear' is imaginary. Once you enter the troubled waters, you realize it is water, like any other water, with a lot of therapeutic value.*
>
> *Nita Agarwal overcame her fear of driving. The fear vanishes the moment you are in the driver's seat. For then you concentrate on driving, and not on your fears!*
>
> *Jaya Gadgil 'sat' in the middle of the road to protect the rights of trees! She overcame the fear of what people will say.*
>
> **(Courtesy: UMANG Spectrum Newsletter, July 2001)**

Freedom from fear helps us in many ways. Fearlessness bestows courage. It helps us take bold decisions, increases efficiency and productivity, bestows peace of mind, creates spaces within and helps in self-growth. It increases sociability and draws people and makes Nature cooperate with us positively.

But let us not miss out on an important fact. Fear has two sides, positive and negative. Principal Gidwani of M.M.K. College, Mumbai drew my attention to the positive aspects of fear. According to him, positive fear has actually helped the society grow, and civilisations to prosper. For example:

- Fear of wild animals has helped man to develop defence systems beginning from crude barriers to houses, tribes and walled cities.

- Parental fears lead to the protection of children.
- Fear of authority, leads to obedience, law and order.
- Fear of losing face, or self-esteem, or fear of criticism builds up inner value systems and character.

Positive fears act as checks/balances in the upswing/downswing of life. J. Krishnamurthy, when asked how to be free from fear, said, "Self is the cause of fear. So long as I am seeking security in any form, there must be fear, from which all the basic urges spring." He further explains the cause of fear as two processes operating within every one of us. One, that wants to 'achieve' something, like happiness. The other which knows the difficulties involved in that, like it is not possible to be very happy. Thus there is a dual process within us. To be free from fear, we must stop this dual process.

And here is a bit of English wisdom:

> *Learn from the past.*
> *Do not come to the end of your life*
> *Only to find you have not lived.*
> *For many come to the point of leaving life*
> *Space of the earth/and when they gaze back,*
> *They see the joy and the beauty that could not be theirs because of the fears they lived.*

Coping With Sorrow

The famous Urdu poet Sahir Ludhianvi writes:-

> *Who in this world has not received sorrow?*
> *Paths leading to ecstasy and agony*
> *Are meant for the whole human progeny*
> *If by sorrow's hand, you lose a battle*
> *Then on all hands, you lose mettle.*

Pleasure and pain, love and sorrow are like the Gemini twins, inseparable. For life is based on the principle of balance and equality. We go through life, with pain and suffering, we are entangled in pleasure lust and desire.

Sorrow plays an important part in our lives. It draws out our strength, moulds our character, and does that finer tuning of ego which makes life much more liveable and loveable.

Yes, it is possible, that an overwhelming sorrow can crush a person, drag him/her into depression, and even push him into suicide. But that is the extreme negative effect of sorrow on a weak personality.

Three real life stories are here to show how tragedy is converted into fulfilling a life's mission of love and beauty.

Miss Parmar, a college student, a dare devil girl, was returning home one day from the college when she banged into a stationary wagon. She died on the spot. Her father, a timber merchant instead of wallowing in grief, started an NGO for road safety. This NGO conducts workshops and surprise checks on traffic control awareness. Thus, he turned his grief into a life saving and life giving organization.

A lady lost her son in an air crash. The boy was young, and was training to become a commercial pilot. His untimely death plunged the mother's heart into a pit of darkness. But only for a while. Soon she joined a children's organization and became a mother to hundreds of destitute children. She converted sorrow into love.

When Renuka died young, her parents were miserable .Then through proverbial Hindu Vedantic wisdom, they did the best thing they could do. They donated a large sum of money, meant for the education/ wedding expenses of their daughter to a school. Thus, they became instrumental in educating hundreds of Renukas. The personal sorrow of parents turned into public benefit for the masses.

By sheer coincidence we have arrived at Nature's secret, The Law of Transformation – *Life's purpose is to unsheathe*

the soul through sorrow, pain and grinding of ego; to prepare it to evolve for the higher things in life such as Eternal Bliss.

Coping with Anger

A month ago I received an email from a corporate head. He wrote, "I get angry very quickly. This creates problems at the workplace. My anger spreads like a wildfire and vitiates the whole environment at the office. Please help me out."

If one were to analyse his problem one would realise that authority brings anger because it gives one the power to control others. Relax the control and you will find no reason to be angry.

Why does one get angry? The reasons can be as many as the leaves on a tree. But the common cause is when things do not turn out as planned, or expected. When an employee makes a mistake, or is arrogant, or when the client is fussy, or when there are delays beyond our control.

Psychologists correlate efficiency with anger negatively. Anger freezes the mind and mists the vision. Anger is one of the most destructive emotions – it destroys the one who gets angry and the one who is the target of anger.

A negative situation should not be met with a negative situation. Sometimes patience and calmness resolve the problem faster than shouting and screaming. Even negotiations are easier done through appreciation and sugar coated words. A positive response to a negative situation melts away the blockages and opens the way for a fruitful dialogue.

So my reply to the above email was:

If you are looking for a permanent solution to your problem of 'fume and fire' then learn to control your mind.

The short term remedies are many, some of which are listed below:

- Take away your mind from the object of your anger
- Take a deep breath and count up to ten
- Divert the mind to another event/incident
- Find a solution to the problem with a relaxed mind rather than doing it while seething with anger
- Learn to forgive the others' mistakes and your own
- Begin the day with positive aspirations
- Take a five minute break every few hours – let your mind travel to beautiful spots; recount happy incidents of your childhood, and top it with a thank you prayer to the Universe.

Coping With Tensions

Tension is like an overplayed music record wearing out the threads of the mind. It is a habit of clinging to one thought, without letting it go. Doctors say that 80 per cent of illnesses are emotionally induced; a substantial percentage of which is caused by tension.

Causes of tension

Negative reaction to the world around us

Change is the law of Nature. The world is continuously changing. Some of us cannot accept this change; others cannot adapt to it. The changes cause a lot of insecurity and uncertainty. The fear of loss, of hardships, of war, of communal disharmony, of general unrest in the world, brings in negative reactions, causing tension. 'What if this happens? What if this happens to me?' That very thought sets a chain of negative reactions.

The 'butterfly mind'

The second cause of tension is the unfocused mind. This is because we are weary with excess activity. We think of several things during the same time. Often we are doing one thing and thinking of another. A cluttered mind is a chaotic mind, inefficient and restless.

Competition in career or at home among siblings
'I have to do it', kind of rigidity, to elevate the ego is a cause of tension. 'One has to have a winning goal' may be alright for some but not for all. The criteria for achieving anything should be whether you enjoy doing it, whether you love doing it, whether you are comfortable with it?

Lack of confidence
Diffidence is the main cause of tension, as it brings in self-doubt, low self esteem, confusion, contradiction etc.

Lack of positive energy
Tension is the reflection of negative energy. A positive person, with his positive energy would disarm any negative thought of self-doubt, incompetence, and the unrest within and without.

Worry
Worry is one of the greatest producers of tension. The more you worry the more tense you become. This dissipates a lot of your energy and you end up crying.

Worry is like a rocking chair. It takes you nowhere but it keeps you occupied.

Tension Busters

Be Single-minded
'One thing at a time and that done well' is a very good rule as many can tell.

Have Priority Preferences

When the mind is moving in multiple directions, give it a 'focus blueprint' by jotting doing your urgency, priority of activities to be done.

Practice half an hour of silence

Fruits of silence are many. Silence relaxes the mind, and tensions fall away.

It opens up the fourth dimension of life. It rejuvenates the mind as it draws energy from the Universal Mind. It brings in answers to many of our problems.

Unburden the tension through dialogue

Confide in someone close to you about the 'troublesome thought'. Unburden the mind; release it of that persistent bite, by going to a counsellor, a friend, spiritual guide or Guru. If you do not find anyone, just talk to God.

Visit a shrine, chapel or a garden with good vibrations

Just a visit to any peaceful place would melt away the tension. Change of environment also works as a check dam.

Music produces pleasant vibrations

Good music is a good mood-manager. It immediately brings peace and relaxation. It changes the thought process.

Reading positive literature

Self-help books, soul-uplifting stories, pithy poems, and biographies of courage are good tension busters, as they empower you to face life with ease and confidence.

Gym workouts

Any physical exercise, even simple walking, refreshes the mind. Physical tiredness induces mental relaxation and sleep.

Mental relaxation

Mental relaxation exercises are described elsewhere in detail in this book.

Faith and Prayer

Faith can move mountains. If you have 'positive' faith that 'this will be done' or 'I will be cured', then the tension melts away into peace and prayer. Says Urmila Ramrakhiani, member of Fruits of Silence, St.Patricks town, Pune, "The prayer gives confidence to overcome whatever one may have to face. I used to suffer from a phobia, my fear of travelling by road. I used to be tense all the time, if I had to go on the road. This fear vanished with prayer, and faith in protection by the Almighty. Now, I enjoy travelling much more, especially long distance. I used to shiver sitting in the passenger seat. Then one day, I sat in a corner and prayed for Guidance. I was asked to learn driving. I did so. Today I am confident behind the steering wheel."

Avoid everyday tensions

There are certain tensions which can be avoided altogether. For example, if you do not like a person, avoid meeting that person. If certain jobs irritate you, delegate them to someone else. There are tensions, day to day, which can be reduced with a slight adjustment. For instance the morning tension of rush, rush, can be reduced by getting up earlier by half an hour. If you have something on your mind, get rid of it by finishing it as soon as possible. If all this fails, remember you have the power within you to change your own attitude towards situations and take them in your stride. Be cool!

Let go

Do not cling to a tension generating thought. Let it go. Substitute it with something more meaningful and more creative. An empty mind is a devil's workshop. Hook your mind to something better and higher. One way of engaging the mind in a constant rhythmic activity is recitation of a mantra or a prayer.

Aids to Positivism and repairing energy, a personal experience
Are you a negative person? Do you go numb with fear? Do you burn with envy? Do you despair easily? Do you go up in smoke at the slightest provocation? Is your subconscious always sliding down the hill? Then take it from me that

you are losing a lot of energy which could have been used to be more productive and efficient.

At every step, at every moment, we are assailed by doubts, fears, uncertainty. At a certain point of life we all face rejection, failure, disappointment and disillusionment. We become prey to negativism, an excess of which can be destructive. It can kill the mind, wrench the heart, hurt the spirit. The balance should be restored before such negativism pulls you down in the dumps.

Is there a way to restore this balance? Yes, there is. Years ago I learnt **my first lesson** in 'repairing' the energy. I was a sensitive person. One day I entered a room filled with people from all walks of life. Immediately I felt nervous. My stomach churned with anxiety as my very being seemed to have received very unpleasant vibrations. I ran out into the open space and sat down under a huge shady tree. I felt totally at peace. The tension was eased. While man is constantly emanating negative energy, nature restores the balance through its positive force. Communing with nature is the best way to achieve positivism.

My second lesson came when I was reading Buddhist literature. By sheer coincidence, I learnt that negative emotional energy can be nullified, through 'retracing of thought'. For example, while getting into a car, you fear an accident, immediately retrace it with positivism, and visualize that you are driving safely. If a negative thought of failure flashes across your mind, retrace or substitute it immediately with success. Psycho-cybernetics is a new concept, but the Enlightened One had taught this to his disciples 2,500 years ago. 'Retracing thought' is the best dam against the flow of negative energy.

While reading the book *Vedic Cosmology*, by Mr. M.K. Talreja I discovered a strange truth. The rituals we so soften ridicule are an exalted source of positivism. Some of the rituals are symbolic and provide an external aid to being positive. For example, lighting the lamp at dusk dispels darkness. Chiming of the temple/church bells wipes off mental cobwebs.

I learnt **my third lesson** at the Sandhya *'arati'* at the Ramakrishna Mission in Bombay. The shrill sound of conch shells, combined with the metallic beat of cymbals, and the thunder of *'dholaks'* cleared away the mental confusion and crossroads I felt right in my head. That was lesson number three. Performing a ritual paves the way for the positive energy to flow in.

It was while combating the negative thoughts, that my Yoga teacher taught me two things. First; anything that integrates body, mind, and soul such as Yoga, meditation, or the knowledge of *Vedanta* is an aid to positive living. Second, follow grandma's times. The 'Lekhni' as it is called subtly, transforms the subconscious mind by introducing positive energy into it. Both these traditional methods have a long term effect. And so I learnt **my fourth lesson** from my Yoga teacher i.e., Yoga and OM are the integrating mechanism for positive living.

The New Age has introduced many new techniques of 'positivising'. The most popular among them, perhaps, is Reiki. Here I learnt lesson number five, let the mind accept every situation. Do not bang your head on the wall, but use it as a prop. Lean against it and feel comfortable.

Positive living brings in not only material success, but also an inner peace and joy, which according to my Guru are the birthright of every human being.

Higher Energy for Health and Happiness

"How do I raise my level of energy?" This question came from a 24 year old man, who was the victim of circumstances over which he had little control. He was caught in a 'negative trap'. In other words, the situation needed immediate attention...

Negative thoughts and emotions drain away energy. Traumas such as a dear one's death, relocation, and sudden disease cause distress and stress, both physical and mental. This results in a vicious circle of negativism that lowers the levels of energy further.

In such a situation, how does one raise one's energy?

The first step is to stop wasting mental energy. A great deal of mental energy is lost in unproductive, weak thinking. On an average, a human being thinks 52,000 to 72,000 thoughts in a day. Seventy per cent of them are vague and weak. Such useless, meaningless thoughts are nebulous like the empty clouds, which do not rain, but hang like cobwebs in the crevices of the mind. These thoughts should be controlled through awareness or through techniques of mind control such as meditation, concentration or backward counting from 50/100/500.

The second step is retracing of negative thoughts to nullify their effect.

Thought is an energy and when this negative energy goes out as a strong thought, it tends to materialize, or tends to happen. Retracing thought is the Buddhist way of neutralizing the negative thought. For instance, if you think that 'today I will be late for work,' substitute it with, 'today I will be on time for work.' In addition, pledge it to your mind. Retrace negative thoughts and substitute them with positive energy. You will feel the space in your mind immediately.

The third step is deep breathing early in the morning and deep breathing at least twenty times in the evening. At sunset, the level of 'sun' energy is very low. There is something called sunset syndrome. It is at sunset hour that we have to replenish energy. That is why we have so many rituals connected with the 'sunset hour' or 'Godhuli' (when the cattle return home at dusk, raising dust in the soft sunlight).

The fourth step is participation in *Arati*. *Arati* is performed with chiming metal bells, beating *'nagaras'* (drums) and loud blowing of conch shells, with a clash of cymbals and flickering flames amidst the aroma of incense sticks. All of which heighten the 'sound' vibrations and 'light' rays. When added up, these vibrations become a great source of energy. One has only to become aware of the vitality of the atmosphere and experience the energy.

The fifth step is to take energy from Nature. Take energy from the 'sun' in the morning by the ritual of pouring water and bowing to this great cosmic ball of fire. Trees are another source of energy. Embrace them and borrow their power of self-generation. Walking in the woods or meditating under trees is very soothing. It also raises the level of energy. Flowers have a healing power; seek their help in smiling away your blues. Trees and flowers are very sensitive to human thought and respond immediately; and can fill you with healing properties.

The sixth step is getting energy through the 'word', read or heard. Reading positive literature dispels negative thoughts and makes room for positive energy to flow in. It is called the 'light of literature.' Fill your mind with the light of literature and all the darkness of negativism will vanish.

The seventh step is the New age Activity. That is, getting energy through crystals, Reiki, gems and precious stones. Reiki and *pranic* healing are cleansing processes. They wipe away the dust of negative thoughts. They provide the direct channel for energy to flow in. As far as gems are concerned, every 'gem' has its own potent quality. For example; amethyst is the source of 'confidence' energy. 'Ruby' is source of solar energy (success energy).

Finally you can raise your energy through *Pranayama*. *Pranayama* removes the imbalances in your body and makes it more receptive to 'breath' energy. Many of the esoteric practices have discovered rhythmic patterns, which immediately raise the energy. One such device is *Sudarshan Kirya*. Many people have benefited by its 'energy' effects. *Pranayama* integrates body, mind and soul and therefore is the holistic way of getting energy from the vast cosmic Infinity.

Auto Suggestions

> More than the power of reflection is the power of suggestion.
> **Sadhu T.L. Vaswani**

Reflection is necessary. Through reflection one arrives at solutions, desired goals, and distant visions. But more than reflection is the power of suggestion. Years ago, I came across an interesting story of a young girl who underwent surgery following an accident. As a result of this one leg became shorter than the other. The surgeon who operated on her, said that nothing could be done about it. This girl did not lose courage. She was determined to overcome this handicap. She decided to work on herself through auto-suggestion.

Every morning she would stand before the mirror and tell herself that her leg is growing and that both the legs are equal in length. She worked on auto suggestion for a few months, and believe it or not, the shorter leg grew to be of the same length as the longer one. Such is the power of auto suggestion.

Regular 'suggestions' becomes cumulative in effect and with their own cumulative power, become transformed into reality. To begin with, every thought is only a suggestion, then it becomes solidified into words or action.

Exercise

Goal – to have a happy day.

Get up in the morning. Before you start on the day's chores keep telling yourself "I am going to have a great day," several times. At first say this silently, and then loudly, may be speak to yourself while looking into a mirror.

Certain prayers are a kind of auto suggestion of positivism. Group prayer is more powerful because of the 'multiplier' effect of the prayer. Group consciousness is more potent than the individual mind.

Anticipating or expectation is also a form of auto suggestion. Remember, it is these signals received by the subconscious mind that brings in the desired results.

Mind Therapies

The Mantra Therapy
A Cure for All Diseases – Physical, Mental and Emotional

The Mantra therapy is my grandmother's prescription for illness. As a child, whenever I had fever, my grandmother used to go to a quiet corner and recite *Sukhmani Saheb*. Then she would dip the corners of the holy cover in a cup of water and give me that holy water to drink. Lo and behold! The fever would vanish in no time. Then I was sceptical of its effect. However, today the physics of Mantra is an open book. My grandmother merely energized the water with *Sukhmani* vibrations.

It is common knowledge, that in case of jaundice, the patient is taken, not to a doctor but to a man who recites a specific mantra for the disease, handed down to him through 'revelation'. There are specialists in this field. They would not give out their secret, even for a price.

To the non-believer, all this may sound like abracadabra. Hold your breath. Every time one calls up any corporate office of the newspaper *Times of India*, *Gayatri Mantra* greets you while you wait for the call to be received. Several other corporate offices have imitated the tune. The popularity of *Gayatri mantra* is due to the advocates of *Kriya yoga* and the Art of Living followers, who believe it to be a stress buster. "*Gayatri Mantra* creates one lakh twenty-five thousand vibrations in your body," explains the advocate of *Kriya yoga*, Mrs. Shashi Khosla. She says, "These vibrations have curative powers as they activate and rejuvenate cells in the body. Every moment the body cells change and renew. The greater the intake of oxygen, the greater the positive effect. And mantra certainly pumps in more oxygen."

According to Swami Vishnu Devananda, "A mantra is mystical energy encased in a sound structure. Every mantra contains within its vibrations a certain power." And it is that power, which energizes a person and heals him. A mantra, though containing words, is so constructed to produce specific vibrations, which potentially are very powerful. We are well aware and physics tells us so, that a 'sound' contains power/energy. The various mantras have been constructed from a combination of sounds to set up specific vibrations. These vibrations when applied scientifically can literally move mountains. These sound vibrations can be manipulated to move physical objects or to move/change human psyche and produce positive effects on the body.

At the spiritual level, they release spiritual energy in the *chakras* of the body. We all know, that sound is the seed of all matter. The Bible says, "In the beginning was the word .Word was with the God."

The beauty of Mantra therapy is that it combines both thought vibrations and sound vibrations. That is why, it is said, that if you recite the *Gayatri mantra* 108 times a day for 'forty days', it can cure diabetes and hypertension. For it changes the mind-psyche and puts you in tune with the Universal psyche. The sound vibrations 'cleanse' the cells and increase the flow of oxygen and energy into the body. It is scientific.

Among the most prominent Vedic mantras are the *beej* (seed) mantras, *Mrityunjay* mantra and of course the *Gayatri* mantra. *Beej* mantras are *Rum, hum, yum*—sounds without words. They work directly on *nadis* and *chakras*. These are recited in various rhythms, cycles and combinations, to produce the various physical, mental and spiritual results. The *beej* mantras, as the name implies are very potent, because like a 'seed' they contain the essence—power of growth. The *beej* mantra when combined with *yoga asanas*, can cure diabetes, kidney and intestine problems, besides producing spiritual effects.

Kriya yoga makes use of these with or without *Pranayama*, with or without *asanas*. *Mrityunjay* mantra, *"Om Triyambakum..."* used to be recited in Ancient India to obtain *Moksha*, but in this age, it is recited during the course of severe illnesses. It is said to be efficacious in warding off ill health, diseases and yes, death! It is recited at the time of surgery, travel and prolonged illness.

Om is a powerful 'cleansing' mantra. It takes away the negativity. *Om* creates vibrations at two important centres in the body—the navel and the spine. *Om*, when combined with *Pranayama yoga*, creates excellent results. It clears the cobwebs of the mind and the 'clogs' in the flow of energy in the body. It provides a healthy mind in a healthy body. It helps in recycling of energy too.

However the mantras have to be recited 'accurately' both for 'psyche change' and 'physical' benefits. The structure of sound should remain specific to produce the required number of vibrations.

It may interest readers to know that all the religions of the world have parallel mantras. For example, Zoroastrians have such powerful verses of *Gathas*, that mere recitation of them can calm the storm. Besides, they have separate prayers for different illnesses etc. Tibetans have mantras for almost everything. The Late Appa Sahib Pant, in his book, *A Moment in Time*, has written how a Lama vanquished rain by reciting a mantra in his presence. The Muslim's *Allah Ho Akbar* also creates vibrations in the body and mind, very similar to *Om*. Its recitation pulls the navel inwards and draws out breath from the stomach, thus relaxing the body and mind by inhaling more oxygen.

Well if Tansen could 'cause' rain by his *Raga Malhar*, and light the lamp with *Raga Deepak*, then the combination of sound and thought—word vibrations could produce many more miracles in our daily life. Why don't you try them?

The Love Therapy

I have been reading a book which has all the possible therapies of the world. However, it does not have the universal therapy—the therapy of Love. Recently, I came across an amazing story of a woman who was healed by the power of love. Shona (name changed) lived alone. One day she fell in the bathroom and injured her arm. Unable to cope up with the situation all by herself, she phoned her best friend for help. The friend came running and took her to an orthopaedic surgeon. On examining the arm, the doctor advised her to take an x-ray of the arm. He suspected a multiple fracture of the humus. Since it was Friday afternoon, the diagnostic clinic in the vicinity had shut by that time and Shona had to wait till Monday for the x-ray to be taken. During that period her friend nursed her with deep love and tender care. Monday evening when Shona visited the same doctor with the x-ray of the arm, he was surprised. It was a miracle he had never witnessed before. The fractured bone had started healing. There was no need for surgery or for setting of the bone. The love and care of the best friend had done what the doctor's medicine would have taken time to do.

Many more cases could be cited of the power of love. Asha, a third year student, staying in a girl's hostel, developed troublesome cough. No amount of medication could help her get rid of it. Out of sheer desperation, the hostel warden sent her off to her local guardian's home.

The cough still persisted. Pathological tests resulted in the doctor advising surgery. A date for the operation of tonsillitis was fixed and her mother was called in from Dubai. Within a week of her mother's arrival, she stopped coughing. The operation was postponed and fresh investigations tested negative. Mother's love had worked wonders.

"Mother's love is pure and unconditional. It can work miracles," says Dr Batra, who practices alternative healing therapies, "Especially distance Reiki, distance crystal healing and therapies using positive energy are more effective with the presence of mother's love, or wife's love." It is the love that matters.

While searching for more medical cases cured by love therapy I met a doctor who confessed, "Love combined with prayer has cured many ills." Many diseases begin in the mind. There are cases where patients develop physical illness because of alienation, emotional starvation, low self-esteem, anomie, loneliness, rejection; fear of failure, death, rejection; loss of face, loss of relatives and friends. These can be treated through love and a sense of belonging.

How does love heal?

"Love warms eases, restores and renews every cell and fills the whole being with joy, peace and well-being. Every smile we give to another warms our hearts, every kind word or act contributes towards setting into action a mighty power and spiritual force within our being; the effect is miraculous.

"Love is a powerful positive energy. Warming of the heart or feeling of love itself can dispel negative energy from body."

Today, psychologists and doctors agree that most diseases have roots in the mind. We may change it to; most of the diseases have roots in emotions/heart. The body, mind and spirit connectivity, works together, synergies together. Love is that vital synergy. "Love is the great cosmic law of creativity." says Sadhu Vaswani.

Since we all know the healing power of love, shouldn't we try it out the next time a dear and near one falls ill? Let's see whether love can make roses bloom on jaundiced faces!

Cinema Therapy

There are many therapies for the much harassed modern man; music therapy, mantra therapy, past life therapy, crystal therapy, and aromatherapy, to name a few. Add to these, the Cinema therapy.

Cinema therapy is perhaps one of the old remedies for stress ridden, mentally troubled and neurotic human beings. We have it on record, that as early as 1938, research study was conducted in Moscow, to find the effect cinema had on a 'certain type' of patients. Consequently, a special cinema studio was built at the Psychiatric Hospital in Podolsk, near Moscow. Experiments carried out on patients showed that under the influence of the quiet rhythm of a film, epileptics became calm and felt better for some days. Violent mental cases, behaved well after watching a light comedy. Laughter is healing and so it is the best medicine.

Cinema therapy means treatment with the aid of films applied to patients suffering from nervous and mental disorders. It works the same way as the mantra or music therapy. It restores the bio-mental rhythm balance and improves the physical and mental health of patients.

Cinema therapy uses Health Films as the medium in treatment of various disorders such as stress, nervousness, fatigue syndrome, alienation and disorientation due to mental tension etc.

Health films are 'light comedy', which have a positive effect on the mind, which cause "laughter" and naturally, the classic example of Health Films, would be the Charlie Chaplin type, which is 'pure comedy', and one laughs at the 'accidental situations' or 'jinxed situations'. 'Light comedy' has many variations. Buffoonery or joker category, may appeal to young minds, but would not find favour with adults undergoing stress. Then there are *sick comedies*. For instance, many films, especially Hindi films have a 'laughter component' hinged on a 'personal deficiency' or an unfamiliar accent, where the 'empathy' of the viewer may actually result in fear or an inferiority complex (For example: A man slipping over a banana skin or a South Indian speaking Hindi in Tamil). Nevertheless, it has been found that movies/TV serials like *Here's Lucy* or *Three stooges* and even *Mind your Language* have a relaxing effect on the mind. On the Indian front, sitcoms such as Jaspal Bhatti's laughter capsules are doubly beneficial, as they relate to day to day problems and also make laughter their business.

Laughter is a great stress buster and tension shooter. Not the forced, imposed or the self-imposed laughter in laughter clubs, but the one which is 'an experience', both visual and emotional. It is an 'imprint on your psyche'. Laughter which is from the within is youthful and rejuvenating, as it invigorates the body cells through better supply of oxygen. (Anything that is tension-free functions better).

Gayatri, the film critic says, "The films do not portray the required role models. And so you find today's youth watching films for time pass" without receiving any relief for their problems of anomie, depression, frustration etc.

Most of the negative emotions, like fear, depression, loneliness, diffidence, and lack of identity are found in a Repressed Personality. They need either the safety valve of catharsis, or a situation with which they can emphasize and yet laugh enough to shed some of the negativism. On the other hand, health films have a semi-permanent effect as they have 'recall value'. They become a part of your memory album and a reference point for creating more laughter.

In this age of technology, we are obsessed with Health—health food, health drink, health exercise. Why not health films?

Managing the Body

What is the most useful activity everyday which we perform? It is breathing!

If you control your 'breathing', you can control the health of the body. On an average human beings breathe 12-20 times per minute. The fewer the breaths one takes, the longer the lifespan. Do you know that tortoise live for hundreds of years? Its breathing rate is as slow as one breath in one minute.

Hence for a healthy body, you must practice deep slow breathing. Right breathing is one of the greatest parameters of good health; slower the breathing, healthier the body. The other necessities are balanced diet,

Pranayama Yoga, and mental and physical exercise.

> *Live thy full span of life,*
> *Welcome old age with delight.*
> **Rigveda**

Balanced Diet

A balanced diet may be defined as an appropriate mix of nutrients, i.e., proteins, carbohydrates, minerals and vitamins. The most important element in a balanced diet is something called 'lisle' which is necessary for integrating proteins in blood. Hence food combinations should be such as to produce enough 'lycil'. Milk and bread is such a combination. A balanced diet is necessarily a combination diet. Women going on 'Diet Therapy' should take note of this, because the food we take should be assimilated in the body. A balanced diet, therefore combines cereals, pulses, vegetables, fruits, meat/fish products and milk/milk products in desirable proportions. A balanced diet adequately meets the needs of the body; keeps it healthy and fit. Most of the regional diet is balanced and suited to the geographical conditions. For instance, *idli*, chutney, *sambhar* cooked with vegetables is balanced food.

Similarly, *dal, bhat* (pulses, rice), *saag* (vegetable), *roti* (*Chapatti*/bread) with curds/*kheer* (thick sweetened milk) is a balanced meal.

Dahi-vada is balanced so is *Kulcha-chhole*.

Yoga and Health

Yoga is a process of integration of body and mind. It has eight *angas* or limbs:

Yama	– ethical observation
Niyama	– good physical and mental habits
Asana	– physical exercises
Pranayamaa	– inhalation/exhalation
Pratihara	– control of mind
Dharana	– concentration
Dhyana	– meditation
Samadhi	– total bliss, illumination

The first five constitute the external yoga, the last three the internal yoga. In this book, we are concerned with those yogic exercises and practices, which will enhance physical beauty, increase vitality and repair bad health. Physiological health of human beings depends upon the regulation of endocrine glands. These ductless glands comprise thyroid, pituitary, pineal, adrenals and ovaries, yielding a powerful effect on the nervous system. They stimulate or depress emotions, and influence the mind and its activities. The regular yogic exercises regulate and control the activities of these glands. *Surya Namaskar* is one such *asana* that helps to regulate the endocrine glands.

Surya Namaskar

It is a complete *asana* as it combines eight *asanas*. It is a prayer to the rising sun. It involves all your limbs, helps in the circulation of blood and stretches the spine, abdomen and stomach. Inhaling and exhaling of breath also helps integrate the limb and mind movement. This *asana* should be performed facing the early morning sun or the setting sun.

Exercise

Every part of our body needs maintenance i.e. every part of the body should be exercised. Here are a few simple exercises for the body

- Walking: Both brisk and slow walks are good exercises. You may walk from one kilometre to five kilometres a day.
- Frog-leap exercise: Sit without a chair. Bend knees, jump like a frog. Do this exercise for a maximum of three to four minutes.
- Wheel Exercise: Lie on your back with hands by your sides and your toes together. Raise your legs above one foot about one foot above the ground. Slowly rotate the legs like a wheel. First rotate from left to right .Follow this with right to left movement. This exercise reduces fat on tummy and buttocks.
- Prayer exercise: Sit on your heels touching the ground. Keep your back straight. Now place your hands in prayer position on your head, keep your back straight. Do this exercise for a few minutes. This exercise is good for your entire body.

Here are suggestions for keeping your mind alert and healthy.

- Practice silence for at least 20 minutes everyday .This will calm your mind.
- Do Suduko for a while
- Play Bridge (card game) or chess
- Solve crossword puzzles

Relaxation

We live in an age of speed and uncertainty. We are running all the time, rushing through life without enjoying it. Every little thing stresses us out resulting in diseases like high blood pressure, nervous disorder and cardiac problems. Every one of us must learn to relax. There are easy ways to bring beauty to life.

Physiological Techniques of Relaxation

Deep breathing

Sit in a comfortable position in a quiet place. Inhale the air deeply, retain the breath for a while and then exhale the air.

- Time the inhalation for 5 seconds, retain the breath for 5 seconds, and exhale for 5 seconds. Do three to five rounds of this.
- Time the inhalation for 5 seconds, retain the breath for seven seconds and exhale for 5 seconds. Do three to five rounds.
- Breathe in slowly in instalments of one second each. If your breathing in takes five seconds, then breath in 1 second, pause 1 second, and so on. Hold the breath for five seconds and then exhale in one go. You may practice this in reverse order. In other words, exhale in instalments and breathe in at one go. Do five rounds of each.

- Breathe in through nostrils but exhale through throat and mouth. Do five rounds of this exercise.

Psychological Techniques of Relaxation

1. Empty the mind

Sometimes the stress is not obvious, and the person looks calm and composed. But there is tension in the subconscious mind. There are several techniques of dispelling or diluting this tension in the subconscious mind. One is to empty your mind of all thoughts. Be blank. Deliberately forget all the unkindness, cruelty, exploitation, hurts, fears, despair, which have caused this tension. Say to yourself, "Today is over. Tomorrow is a fresh day." Begin the next day as a fresh day.

2. Reinforce

Much of mental tension and work stress is caused by self doubt, diffidence, inhibition and unknown fears. Steer out of this situation, by suggesting to yourself confidence, boldness and success. "Reinforce" your mind, with instances of success and love or other areas where you have felt comfortable. Think over these areas where the signals are positive. Checklist your assets; add positive points in your personality. Repeat them to yourself in order to build a healthy ego. Reinforcement of positive assets will gradually erase the negative imprints on the subconscious mind. Moreover, you are bound to feel good.

3. 'Psycho-cyber nets' Technique of Relaxation

First sit in a quiet place. Breathe correctly and naturally. Completely do away with any kind of ill thoughts. Imagine yourself to be relaxed. Visualize yourself as the next person.

Experience being relaxed. Make yourself believe you are relaxed. Make sure you are really relaxed.

4. Psychological tension busters
Sit quietly. Close your eyes. Imagine you are in an art gallery. You are in a torso statue put on a pedestal. People are moving around it. So you are you. You are seeing you own statue- hair, eyes, nose, lips, etc. objectively as someone in the crowd. Admire it. Criticize it. Accept it as one of the pieces on view. This will give you objectivity and detachment from self.

Common Methods of Relaxation
Take a leisurely stroll in the evening. Do a five minute exercise after returning from work. Have a good shower after a strenuous day or work. Divert your mind with a magazine/glossy/joke book. Play soft music. Relax with a hobby at the end of the day. Call up your best friend. Relax with a drink. Just, sit in a chair and think nothing. Play a game of cards/a game of snakes and ladders with family. Relax with prayer, as they say, "A family that prays together stays together".

Hurdle crossing Meditation
Mr. Jayesh Shah of Humanist Movement in Mumbai once conducted a meditation session in my house. We were just a small gathering, he gave us a leaflet that was to be read by one person while all the others in the room had to relax, with their eyes closed and concentrate on the paragraph being read. I experimented with this unique meditation on my students in St. Mira's College for girls in the year 1998. This experiment proved to be successful.

Here is an excerpt from the 'reading':

> *'You are on the bank of a small stream; you want to cross it because beyond this there is a road that passes through forests and deserts to reach the mountaintop. There is a bright light– may be a temple, may be a church. You want to reach there.*
>
> *You are contemplating on how to cross the river, and a boat comes by. You sit in the boat and cross over. You begin to take the path that goes to the mountain path. It is dark. The forest looks forbidding. You confront the fear, the great fear of being eaten alive by wild animals. You are tired and thirsty. You scan for a forest rest house. You are at the end of your tether. When you have almost given up, you sight a flicker of light. A very thin beam of light. You wonder whether it is an illusion or reality. You trudge on. That flicker of light is your only hope. You crunch on the dry leaves, push aside the silvery roots of banyan trees, pull away the tangle of things – this too shall pass away. You sight a hut.*
>
> *There inside the hut is a tiny wicker lamp. In it's light you see an old man. He gives a beautiful smile. You heave a sigh of relief. There is a pitcher of water to slake your thirst and some fruits to free you from pangs of hunger. You rest for a while. Next morning you begin your trek early. For the mountaintop is far, and you have to climb all the way. The ascent is tiring. You are fagged out, low in body, mind and spirit. And there, lo and behold, there is a tiny stream and a gorgeous waterfall! You drink the cool water of the rivulet and bathe in the icy waterfall. You are rejuvenated and you continue the climb once again. At last, you reach the mountaintop.*
>
> **This passage is an adaptation of the 'meditation' reading available with the Humanist Movement.**

What did you experience?

Relax the mind and body. Relax the body; mind will be relieved of tension. Relax both for success. Relaxation is the rhythm of life. Happiness lies in the rhythm of life.

MANAGING RELATIONSHIPS

How to Build Good Relationships

There is an eternal law of the universe. We reap what we sow. Our relationships are what we make of them. Good human relations are the art and science of making our relationships with one another, a mutually satisfying experience. Psychologists are of the opinion that the keys to human relations are two. The first of these is the needs and the habits of the personality we must develop in order to satisfy these needs, and thus make our relationships satisfying to the other person as well as to us.

Basically as a human being other people are the same as we are. The chief motivations of their behaviour are their integral hungers, just as ours are to us. Their hunger to be treated as a human being is just as it is ours. Their hunger to be 'needed' and wanted, to love and to be loved is just as it is ours. To relate ourselves to others in ways that satisfy these hungers is to make any relationship mutually satisfying. It is the essence of good relationships.

Good human relations play an important role in creating happiness. Even our ancient scriptures carry guidance for the 'inputs' required to make life meaningful and satisfying. One of the most important inputs is a friendly attitude.

Friendly attitude

> Let us look at all, with friendly eyes
> May all look at me, with friendly eyes
> May I look at all with friendly eyes
> May all look at one another with a friendly eye.

Scriptures urge us to be friendly, because then there will be no hatred, no animosity, no disturbing elements in our relationships. However, a friendly attitude does not mean flashing a smile at people and showing pearly teeth to an audience or an assembly.

What is friendly attitude?

To have a friendly attitude is to respect the sentiments of others, be communicative, quietly assuring, courteous, helpful, considerate, kind, compassionate, loving and sympathetic.

According to Acharya Mahaprajna, "The person who has not developed friendliness has an underdeveloped morale. Enmity is so poisonous that it keeps troubling and weakening the morale of whomsoever it infects, creating frustration, depression, weakness, jealousy and dejection."

No man is an island unto himself. He lives in society. He is part of human relationships that society weaves around him with its norms, binds, and blood connectivity network. Every person wants the warmth of friendliness, fellowship of men. Every person needs respect, and acceptability.

This feeling of friendliness will come naturally when we take a broader view of the universe and realize that we are all equal, children of the same planet earth, and we share the same air, earth, and sky. That we are made in the 'image of god', that brotherhood is the essence of living and loving; that we are one.

How to Build Good Relationships 63

Let me narrate an incident from the life of Mother Teresa. While she was collecting money for one of her noble causes, a beggar woman went up to her with a ten paisa coin and said, "This is my contribution to your cause". Mother Teresa accepted the ten paisa coin with gratitude. The beggar woman was so poor, that it almost broke her heart to accept that 'money'. But she did not want to hurt her. She recognized and acknowledged the pride and dignity of the poor beggar woman.

Mother Teresa made the beggar woman feel 'human', the one who was capable of contributing however little to a great cause.

A person who sows the seeds of friendliness reaps a rich harvest of happiness.

An important thing is to acknowledge people around you. Remember them by wishing them on their birthdays, give them gifts of home cooked food or just the warmth of love. Greet people with a smile.

Be a popular role model

It is a common saying, "Do unto others, as you would like others to do unto you!" For that, you have to be a role model for others. A beautiful verse by Osho conveys it well.

> You can do something,
> For the human being that you are.
> Drop all conflicting tendencies:
> Violence, aggression, fear.
> Be loving, prayerful, meditative.
> Create at least one human being as you like the whole humanity to be.
> At least create a model within you
> So your fragrance spreads...

It is up to you to create a niche for yourself in society. You have to extend a helping hand, you have to adopt people, rather than people adopting you! In our family, the social role model is an uncle, Mr. Chandru Kamlani, popularly known as 'Bhau'. He is an icon of help and love. Bhau has a way of adopting people. His five well known traits are:

- Extend a helping hand wherever and whenever required.
- Try to become one with the local people.
- Do good to all, irrespective of caste, creed, religion, or family; without any expectations.
- Protect the weak and those who are suffering.
- Consider the world as your own (family).

The prayer of Shanti Deva is a good example:

> May I be for all who ail,
> A doctor, a nurse,
> May I be to those who long for
> The other shore, a boat, a bridge!

You have to change your attitude. You have to move out of yourself to others. Avoid gossiping, backbiting, envy, jealousy, and the tit for tat attitude.

Social Health

We are so obsessed with our own health, and with our relationship with the self that we forget that we are a part and parcel of society. An individual human being is as much an integral part of society as leaves are of a tree. An individual leaf cannot survive without the tree to which it belongs.

Family

Family values are in. So are Asian values. Written thousands of years ago the *Atharvaveda* referred to ideal family bonding as –

> May son follow
> The footsteps of his father
> May he have unity of mind
> With his mother,
> May wife talk to her husband,
> In gentle words, as sweet as honey.

Five simple rules of family bonding:

1. *Be in touch, be connected*

With instant communication, it is so easy to be connected. The beauty of the Indian joint family is that it is scattered in space, but united in time. A regular phone call to the members of the family, an occasional letter and frequent e-mails help to remain in touch.

2. *Be a part of family decisions*

Every family should have an unwritten norm that members must participate in family decisions. These decisions may pertain to career, finance, travel, marriage, allocation of duties and responsibilities in case of illness etc. Family decisions should always be taken jointly.

3. *Remember important events in the family*

Try to remember birthdays and other important events of the family members. Make your relationship a celebration of events, a phone call, a greeting card or a bouquet, go a long way in keeping you happily connected. Keep a wedding anniversary, birthday and events diary. Make it your prayer book; open it every morning for action.

4. *Gifting and giving*

Gifting is an expression of joy, self and love. In India 'gifting' was an informal affair till recently. Gifting from parents and relatives meant giving a ten or a fifty rupee note. It had no packaging, no frills. It needed no selection. Gifting also meant, just giving 'something' to someone. However, the western idea of gifting is totally different. It means buying a special gift, gift wrapping it, and showcasing it as very 'special'. I however, differ with this modern concept. To me gifting is symbolic of giving. Giving can be anything. It is not measured in terms of money, size, visibility. It is the thought behind the action, and not the content. A flower, a plant or a greeting card given with love are more precious than formalized gifts.

5. *Bonding vacations*

Bonding holidays, festivals and ceremonies are important. Family holidays are great fun, though they do require adjustments. A family get together for picnics, important festivals, and ceremonies definitely keep the family connected, bonded and secured. There is a sense of fun, joy and security in such bonding.

Neighbourhood

An old Sindhi proverb says: "The neighbourhood is your mother and father." In Germany, there are unwritten rules for right side neighbour and for left side neighbour. Germany for a long time advocated 'face to face' community—a community which had face-to-face interaction.

Apart from the friendly relationship, every neighbourhood should be a cultural unit. It is heartening that most co-operative societies or modern colonies have either a cultural centre or a club house. The residents meet together on 15th August or 26th January for dinner and entertainment.

Neighbourhoods can become active through associations. For instance in the area we live, Kalyani Nagar, Pune, we have Kalyani Nagar Residents Association, which performs multifarious functions, all aiming at the same target – a cohesive neighbourhood with health and harmony. Cultural events, a quarterly magazine and interactive activities make Kalyani Nagar, truly an ideal neighbourhood. Kalyani Nagar also has a Senior Citizens' Club, a Laughing Club, a Morning Walkers' Group, Three Kitty Groups and Society Associations. It is a neighbourhood which is like an erstwhile village of extended family.

Community bonds to roots

Community is a larger neighbourhood. Community also means an association of a church, a temple or a religious mission. Community in sociological terms refers to socio-religious unit. Every community has certain bonding programmes. Communities which are spread globally, such as Jews, Sindhis and Parsis have associations for interaction, for celebration of their identity. Thus involvement in these activities keeps you in touch with your roots – saves you from that sickening feeling of 'anomie'.

The Nation

Answer the following questions honestly:
- What's your contribution to the Nation?
- Specifically what's your contribution to its development?
- What's your contribution to the political opinion?
- How good a citizen are you?

Whatever your answers, remember you have to be involved with your nation. Your involvement should be active and not passive.

The Human Equation

The ability to treat everyone at par with oneself. Although Vedanta proclaims, 'All in one, and One in All, we do not treat others as ourselves. We do not even treat them at par with ourselves.'

A small child and an elderly man were standing at a stationery shop. The elderly man pushed the child away to pay his bill at the counter. The child in his innocence asked, "Why did you push me?"

The elderly man had no answer.

The late Rukmani Arundale narrated an incident to the students at Pune. She said, "What has happened to the younger generation? I was holding two handbags and tiptoeing my way down the gangway in an aircraft, when the young chap behind me said, 'Can't you move a bit faster?' He should have helped me with the bags. Instead he pushed me aside and said, 'Lady move on. No reverence for age, no reverence for culture'."

On the positive side there is this story from Sadhu Vaswani's childhood. He was fond of playing with the sweeper's son. Once his mother caught him and reprimanded, "Don't you ever touch him!" His innocent reply was, "Mother, isn't he too my brother?"

Raj Kapoor, the great Indian actor, had one advice for his family. "He is truly great who does not think others to be inferior."

Children have a wonderful capacity for treating everyone at par with themselves. It is we adults who put up barriers, barbed wires, walls, etc.

Wearing Masks? How many?

One lesson I learnt from Siddhartha, my husband's nephew is, "Don't force yourself into anything." He has four reasons for it:

- Forcing yourself into anything is violence, and violating of self is destructive.
- Forcing oneself to do anything, like studying, or going to a movie, makes you inattentive; and studying or watching a movie, becomes a burden rather than a pleasure.
- Forcing yourself makes you unnatural and therefore it causes conflict within.
- Forcing yourself reduces efficiency as it is filled with tension.

"Be natural and spontaneous," says the philosopher. To be natural and spontaneous does not mean you have to be wild and untrained. It does not mean that you can be permissive, without any regard for social conduct and disposition. Or that you can do whatever you please.

No, far from it, 'Be natural' means do not wear a mask. We wear masks of different kinds and different types. Our masks, worn one over the other make us 'grotesque', pretentious and bad actors. Masks take away our credibility.

Some masks are so thin and transparent, that even keeping up a 'poker face' doesn't work. It puts us in the docks – dark and demanding. Some masks are thick, so thick, that they crumble under their own weight. Some masks crack and add ugliness to our good natural self.

Being natural takes away so many impeding mental barriers, so many burdens, so many inner controversies and battles. Being natural and spontaneous brings peace, warmth, love and emotional wealth which we can't afford to throw away in the garbage bin. Masks are good for Kathakali dance, Bhutanese folk festivals, and theatre props. Masks for human beings, pretending to be what they are not, are guilt-harvesters. Peel them off before they bruise your skin.

Some people wear masks to enhance their image, they play double role, triple role. If the scene is very demanding masks will leave behind fatigue and futility. True colours, no matter how loud, are better than the grisly, painted, garish gorgon.

We all know the grandma's tale about a wolf in sheep's clothing. Don't we? A cunning wolf thought that it could get the best of meals – sheep, if he mingled with them. So wearing a sheep's coat, it joined a flock of sheep. He would gobble the little ones on the sly, he thought cleverly. As the flock moved from one meadow to another, the sheep bleat and so did the wolf. The shepherd immediately spotted the wolf, and drove him away. The wolf's mask did not pay it well. There is a saying in Sindhi, "Oh Allah, do not make me too clever. The clever have to suffer pain." Let's not be clever like that wolf. If we are sheep, let's remain sheep.

Not by Appearance Alone

I stepped into a wayside shop to buy a raincoat for my young daughter. The rainy season had begun and she was without a raincoat. The shop had a messy look, with cartons of underwear and rainwear piled up everywhere. The salesman, who was inside the living room behind the shop, took ten minutes to come out. I muttered a few words as he slowly walked in, wearing a shabby white pajama and a torn T-shirt. I was getting impatient, as I had the rickshaw waiting outside. One by one he showed me cheap plastic raincoats. I picked up one and asked him to pack it quickly. He did so. Then as he handed me the packet, he smiled, "Aren't you Miss H?" Shocked, I turned away. As I was about to leave, he said, "We were together at the university. Don't you remember me?" We exchanged notes, and I discovered he had spent three years at a Russian University on the Nehru fellowship. Not only that, he had completed his Ph.D. thesis in Social Anthropology and still held a UGC fellowship.

"What are you doing here?" I asked surprised.

"This is our family business. I lend a helping hand in the morning!"

This incident taught me a great lesson in life. Do not go by face value. Looks are deceptive. Misleading.

Swami Krishnanadji used to narrate the following story to us:

> *I was camping in Rishikesh. One day I wanted to distribute food packets to the small colony of beggars on the hillside. Most of them were lepers. As I finished dishing out the food I casually asked, 'Is anyone left out?' 'Yes', came the reply, 'you haven't given food to Baba, who lives up in a hut.' I took the food, trudging up the stony path leading to the hut. Sitting inside was a leper swathed in rags. I requested him to come out and accept the alms. To which he replied in chaste English, 'Won't you come inside and share a meal with me?' That Baba was no ordinary being. He was a great scholar and knew French and German. He had retired as a government officer of a high rank. He was socially*

> ostracized after this attack of leprosy. His family had forsaken him. He had turned to God. He was an 'advanced soul', who chose to live in a beggar colony in Rishikesh.
>
> Swamiji used to warn us, "Don't go by face value. A good coin may be as fake as a tarnished coin may be genuine or made of gold."

Relationship with others is easy

We have heard of the wonder man of 20th century Albert Schweitzer. He was a medical missionary, an established organist and musician, a great thinker and philosopher, besides being an adventurer in the thick jungles of Africa. In spite of being so great, he was still in search of a 'truth' that would build up the civilization in fellowship. That truth came to him while he was going on a barge down the Ogoome River. It was here that the 'truth' flashed through his mind. The truth was *'Reverence for life'*. This was the statement of truth he had been looking for.

Truly, Reverence for all life is the key to the relationship with others. It brings secularity which is the essence of the Truth. It is the secret formula for the art of living with others. *"Vasudhaiva Kutumbakam"* or 'All creation is one family', is our Vedantic heritage. When we respect every creature, small or large, low or high, we express an 'emotional link' with it. This emotion helps us to give and not to take, to create and not to destroy, to strengthen and not to weaken our relationship with others.

The human heart is a source of great love. The emotion of reverence turns into kindness and then into love which is all encompassing. As it has been said, "Emotions are not meant for the luxury of self-indulgence. Emotions should take us out of ourselves." Reaching out to others is much easier with the reverence for all life in our hearts.

We have all heard the story of an ant which killed the mighty pachyderm. When we compare an ant with an elephant, the chasm in their power and physical strength is only too obvious. Yet, an ant, that tiny creature so often walked over has the power to kill the huge robust elephant, thousand million times larger than itself. The moral of the story—do not underestimate anyone. Respect and show reverence even for the most insignificant person.

I am reminded of a student who came from a very humble family. Her father was an office peon, a class IV employee. No one in their wildest dreams had imagined that this girl would reach the top rungs of her profession. Those who sniggered at her ambition, pride and confidence, had to salute her courage and acknowledge her. The very same people who looked down upon her had to seek her help for their own personal and professional needs.

Do not ever underestimate anyone. Every human being has a potential greater than yours. The world is full of talent, genius and there is the universal IQ to help them. Underestimating someone is actually overestimating oneself. Overestimating or overrating oneself is a neurotic complex—an indicator of personality imbalance. When we deal with others there is no need to boast about one's own superiority. We have to treat everyone as an equal.

One man may gaze at a landscape and find no beauty in it. Another may look at it and experience great beauty. To some people even a forest looks ugly because of the fear of insects, reptiles and other creepy crawlies. To others even a desert with shifting sand dunes may look very exciting. It is within us to perceive the good, the beautiful and the loveable; just as it is within us to criticize, abuse and quarrel with others. The problem with us is that we are all confined to the three dimensional world—which is limited. In that limited world, we create our own small world, in which criticizing, fault finding and calling names is accepted. We need to step out of this limited world.

It takes all kinds of people to make this world. It is up to us how we behave. You cannot change people's reactions to you but you can certainly change yours to others.

All relationships are give and take. In the family you have to give more than you take. You have to sacrifice. Even among friends, you have to give more than take. For any relationship to be successful it has to be the above *quid pro quo*.

I remember a story I read in my childhood.

> A young American girl was dancing at New Year's Eve party in a hotel at New York. There she met a young handsome man and fell in love with him. After meeting for some days they decided to get married. The young man warned the girl that he lived in the interior of Alaska. That it was a remote place. But as the saying goes, 'love is blind'. They got married in a church and left for Alaska. There the girl felt isolated. She was used to a different lifestyle which had parties, picnics and branded clothes. Life in that Alaskan town was dull and slow. She could not adjust to her new situation. She decided to go back to the fast track life of New York. Her husband willingly let her go. He took her to the nearest railhead. It was a lonely station with only the two of them on the platform. The train (two compartments) arrived and the girl got into it. As the train left the platform, she waved out to her husband. Then, probably unable to see her go her husband turned his back. As the train chugged forward, the girl saw the receding back of her husband on the deserted lonely platform. Suddenly she realized how lonely her husband would be in that snow bound forlorn place without her. Back in New York, the scene of the receding figure of the husband in that lonely deserted place kept haunting her.
>
> Within a week she was back in Alaska with her husband. Rightly said, love is like a red rose—full of sacrifice.

> Today many marriages are what we call 'distance marriages'. In this category we have 'weekend' and 'month-end' marriages. I had a 'weekend' marriage for several years. My husband used to work in Ahmednagar and I because of my job and our daughter could not go there. Throughout the week I concentrated on my job and our daughter's studies. We had wonderful weekends together as a family and it in no way came in the way of our relationship. Recently I met an IDBI senior executive who worked in Pune, and her husband and children lived in Delhi. "Don't your children miss you?", I asked. "No", was the answer, "I talk to them everyday for half an hour. Besides they live with their grandparents and are fully taken care of." She visited Delhi every month for a weekend. Her husband too visited her once a month. "It is fun and works very well", she said.
>
> **Any relationship built on trust, loyalty and sincerity works well.**

Love Story

We were holidaying in Panchgani, a small hill station in Maharashtra. Our telephone had conked off. I went to an STD shop in the marketplace to call my husband. Waiting in the crowded room for my turn, I saw an attractive young brunette enter. Taking a quick look around, she went to the counter to book her call and then came and sat next to me.

We got talking. She came from a small town in Canada. Her parents were teachers in a missionary school. She was on a spiritual visit to India, she said as she was keen to make 'progress'. After a stint of voluntary work in Kodi, she was in Panchgani to teach in a school.

"I have come to telephone my boyfriend", she confided smiling. "He works in a village in Congo, with underprivileged children." She then proceeded to narrate her love story.

"We both have a similar background. We both aspire to do God's good work. We both love each other deeply. He has proposed to me, but I am hesitant to accept it. I need time. I have come to India in search of the 'Self'. I wanted to give myself six months before giving him my reply. Her beauteous smile and brown eyes gave a radiance to her face difficult to describe.

"Have you found the answer?" I asked.

"Yes and no. Perhaps you can help me", she said, gently holding my hand.

"Me ?" I wondered at her trust and frankness.

"Right now I am focused on my spiritual journey. It is an inner calling. Marriage, I am told, will be an obstacle."

"No, no" I blurted out, "On the contrary, if you two are of the same kind, if you are soul mates, your journey will be faster, easier and beautiful." She took a minute to reflect and accept it. At that juncture her call came through and she rushed to take it. I could hear her holler, "Leo, I love you. Leo, I Love you. Yes, Yes, Yes."

She came out of the booth excited. "Oh, the impossible has happened. I was at last able to get through to that far off village in Africa. It is a miracle. I could talk to him." she said to no one in particular. Then coming over to my side, she whispered, "I have said 'Yes' to him. Next month I shall go to Congo to be engaged. Then together we shall go to Canada where we will be married. Together we will return to Congo, to fulfil the promise of love."

Though this happened a few years ago I can still hear her in the silence of a starry night, "Leo, I love you."

My love is like a red red rose. Red is the colour of sacrifice.

SUCCESS WITH CAREER

For a Successful Career...

We are often advised to choose our career carefully. According to psychologists, the right career is the one for which you have an aptitude. I beg to differ.

My daughter went for an aptitude test after passing her 12th standard. The career counsellor advised her to take up Mechanical Engineering. She however, opted for commerce, completed her MBA and also qualified to be a Kathak dance teacher! I for one have no aptitude for commerce, but by default have taught economics for 35 years in Commerce Colleges! And I feel I have done a fairly a good job of it. Yet, we must respect the 'Success' dictum!

Choose the right career, be in the right job, in the right place/position, at the right time and success is guaranteed! For many whom luck has favoured in climbing to the top position, things have been easy. They just fly from 'Peak to Peak'.

On the other hand, many people struggle hard and get nowhere. There are people who change their career midlife, when they realize they have other abilities and capabilities. My friend Dr. S.Parchani studied to be a linguist. After acquiring a PhD in the subject, she felt she could be better as a social entrepreneur. She successfully opened several socio-economic associations.

Even the glamour world of cinema has many personalities who studied to be doctors or company CEOs.

Dr. Shriram Lagu and Dr. Mohan Agashe trained to be doctors, but found their calling in the moving image of cinema. Ashwini Bhide Deshpande an engineer by profession, has become a renowned classical vocal singer. Dr. Anil Awchat a doctor is a well-known writer and a painter.

A student who did her MBA with flying colours gave it up all for selling chocolates from home. Another student who qualified to teach commerce, went on to become a journalist as it was more to her liking.

The idea is not to confuse you, but to draw your attention to the fact that whatever job/career you choose, you should be able to enjoy it. It is only when you give 101% of yourself to a job, can you enjoy it.

For success in the corporate world, you have to be result oriented. It does not matter whether you are from a vernacular medium school or from an elitist English Medium school. What matters is one's overall personality and the ability to deliver the goods!

There are many examples of world famous industrialists who have had very little formal education. Einstein was a back bencher. Bill Gates left his studies midway due to extenuating circumstances. Both have shown brilliance in their own way. I know at least two industrialists [names withheld for privacy] who schooled in vernacular medium up to the second standard. They succeeded using home wisdom intuitively. Both own businesses of thousand billion dollars.

Education does not mean academic qualifications. Of course, a good academic qualification is a passport to get an entry into the chosen vocation. But it merely assures the entry, and not success. Besides academic education there are many other ingredients required for that delicious taste called success. Believe me they had no mentors. Their main strength was self reliance. Here I would like to quote Dr. Abdul Kalam the former President of India.

> *Self reliance is a path to freedom*
> *Freedom is strength*
> *Strength is more strength*

Career Management Essentials

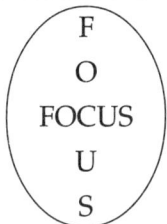

The above chart was prominently placed, not in a corporate office, but in a Holy man's humble house. "It is the complete 'mantra' for success", he said. Whatever work you are doing or want to do, be focused on it. Do not divert your attention to other insignificant things. Be focused on your goal.

It is a complete mantra because:

F – Focus

O – Optimism

C – Confidence

U – Understanding

S – *Shakti* within

Be focused, optimistic, confident, understanding and awaken the *shakti* within.

In each one of us lies tremendous *shakti*. Call it spiritual strength/power, once this *Shakti* is awakened, you can fly from peak to peak.

The spiritual quotient is a matter of:
- Fearlessness – Freedom from mental and physical fears
- Faith – Faith either in oneself, or in the Almighty.
- Focus – A fixed goal, to which your energies should be directed.

Success through AIR

Knowledge has increased. Information has multiplied. In the labyrinth of so much information, one is left groping in the dark. How should one go about using knowledge to one's advantage? Knowledge by itself is like an engine without oil. Knowledge is to be applied, and made into technology.

The most common example is that of water boiling to form steam. For hundreds of years man must have watched this phenomenon, but only one man thought of its 'application'. Steam energy can move things, even move engines and trains. Application of your observations and research can give you a 'breakthrough' in your life and bring tremendous success to you.

When we were in school, we were taught the principle, 'Best from waste'. Beautiful articles were made out of things that are usually discarded. At a flower show held recently in Pune, I saw a most beautiful flower arrangement. It was in an old kettle which most people would have thrown away. The owner won the first prize at the show because she had used her innovative skills to put together an attractive arrangement out of an old kettle and other miscellaneous things.

Innovation means doing something different .You can do something *'hat ke'*(different from the routine) break the existing pattern, be it of thought , of a product, or of a concept. Innovation brings not only success but material awards as well!

So many of us get frustrated and think in circles when a problem comes up. Recently, I gave the job of finding two addresses to two different girls. One of them found the address within a day. She thought of different people who would have the address or would provide her with a clue. She was resourceful enough to contact people, and think of other possibilities. Within 24 hours she could complete the job efficiently. The other girl looked up the phone directory and could not locate the given address. She complained that after spending two hours browsing through the directory, she could not find the said address. Her efforts and time were totally wasted. She was then given a few possibilities to try. She tried reluctantly the next day and wasted half a day searching old files, which probably would have had the address. The third day, she was still stuck with the same job. It was on the fourth day that by chance she came across a person who could guide her to the address.

The first girl was resourceful. She was a go-getter. The second girl, wasted four days in just locating one address. Resourcefulness is a mark of efficiency and success. Have you heard about turn around management? There was this sick unit in one of the MIDC areas near Pune. The company was following the same system of organization and production for almost a decade.

When the CEO of the company retired, a new one was appointed. He completely changed the profile of the company. He did so by re-inventing. He studied the pattern of working of the company. He did some 'fresh' thinking. He reengineered the various functions—marketing, production, HRD and administration of the said company. He 'reinvented' the company. In simple words he had a 'fresh' look at each and every activity of the company, changed them, coordinated them, and successfully brought the ill/dying unit to health and happiness. Due to this reinvention the company made huge profits, distributed heavy bonuses and also organised free celebrative lunches.

Re-engineering is the key to success.

Time Management

We often complain that we have no time. The fact is that we do not know how to manage our time. Besides, there is the famous Parkinson's law which says 'work expands to fill time'.

Time is a human concept. It is a continuous flow. Time lost is lost for ever. You cannot get it back. Hence time is to be used carefully. The question is how to use time to the optimum.

- Make a 'to do' list.
- Arrange it according to priority.
- Have the will power to complete the jobs on hand.
- Avoid wasting time in between; or brooding over the inability to do work.
- Keep some time for relaxation, and for daily exercise/walk/gym.

There is a common saying: *The past is a cancelled cheque; the future is a promissory note; the present is hard cash; make use of it.*

Efficiency through the power of Now

The human mind is like a shuttlecock on the badminton court. It shuttles between the past and the future. It does not rest on the present. The great Indian poet Kalidas has said,

> *For yesterday is but a dream,*
> *And tomorrow is only a vision.*

While we are working in the kitchen, or taking a bath or even driving, our conscious thoughts travel far away, either to what we have done or to what we have to do. While we do our daily chores unconsciously, thanks to the automatic nervous system, our conscious thoughts move here and there, and of regrets, distress or joy as the ease may be pertaining or the past; or the thoughts run to future fears, plans and anxiety of fulfilling them. Very few of us live in the 'Present Moment'. This distracted mind takes away efficiency. Being in the present makes us not only more efficient but saves a lot of energy too.

Henry Van Dyke writes, *"You spend so much time fretting about the past and things that cannot be changed and worrying about the Future and the things which may never happen, that you lose the joy and fullness of now, the present."*

Exercise:
- Be aware of the thoughts floating in the mind.
- When thoughts run backward to the past, bring them forward to the present moment.
- When thoughts rush ahead into the future, then pull them back to the present moment.
- Do this several times a day, till it becomes a habit of the mind.

> *Act, act in the living present*
> *Heart within and God overhead*
>
> **Longfellow**

Old Wine Of Success

Among the many autobiographies and biographies I have read, I have been inspired by the life of JRD Tata.

Jamshetji Tata: His Seven Secrets

It was a vision like that of Kahlil Gibran which made Tata the first industrial leader of India. The vision alone is not sufficient for success. It is to be accompanied by action. And action requires courage.

We can therefore list here the 'seven secrets' of that great industrial seer, who roamed the tiger infested tribal areas of Madhya Pradesh, carrying a stick and a hurricane lantern to launch India's modernization missile. And he did it with a bang!

The great vision

Jamshetji Tata had the conviction of a great visionary. He was sure that India could return to its ancient golden period, when it was heralded as the 'land of milk and honey'. Somewhere he was aware of the great potential this country had for development and industrialization. If a small country like England could launch the Industrial Revolution, why not India with its abundance of mineral wealth, water and manpower.

The creative genius
Jamshetji Tata had the creativity to convert 'sand into gold'. This he proved by converting a marshy land along the Nagpur railway track into a goldmine. 'The earth can yield in abundance, if suitably used,' it was the 'application of the mind' which led to the success of development of his Nagpur Plan.

The ultimate courage
Jamshetji Tata was a daredevil. Of him Jawaharlal Nehru, the late Prime Minister of India has this to say, "When you have to give the lead in action, in ideas—a lead which does not fit in with the very climate of opinion, that is true courage…and it is this type of courage and vision that Jamshetji Tata showed ….." . Such courage is born out of inner conviction.

The adventure of action
Dreams come true only when converted into action. Jamshetji Tata was a man of action. Sir Stanley Reed said, "He conveyed to my mind the impression of the energy and force of a man of action." He was a Karmayogi, a Tapasvi, who believed in action.

Thirst for knowledge
Ultimately it is that part of knowledge that takes you across to your goal. Jamshetji Tata, was a great reader, a great learner. He never missed an opportunity to learn about new things. He explored every possibility, caught every opportunity to do new things. He even studied botany so that he could plant varieties of trees and flowers, and create a pleasant environment. When the Bubonic plague broke out, he studied the causes and the remedies for the same. He dispensed the 'medicines', thus putting his knowledge into practice.

Patience

Jamshetji Tata was ever in command of his situation. He had great patience. Mr.Norman used to say, "I did not see Mr. Tata impatient or intolerant ...". His patience lead to perseverance. It is this quality that makes an industrial leader a great success—The attitude to never, never give up.

Humanity

Jamshetji Tata was down to earth and very humane. He pioneered labour reforms in the country and looked after his employees like a patriarch. He was above caste, creed and community. He was connected with many welfare programmes and schemes. He was the first industrial leader to pioneer environmental programmes for the country.

It will not be out of place to point out here that Mr. Tata followed the secret (subtle) laws of success. To name a few of the ideals he followed:

- The Law of Benefit – He created wealth not for himself alone but for others
- The Law of Giving – What you give returns to you
- The Law of being Thankful – Acknowledgement of gratitude
- The Law of Sacrifice
- The Law of Faith
- The Law of Truth – Honesty and Transparency
- The Law of Equality – The Vedantic human equation

A tribute to J R D Tata describes him as,

> He touched the sky and it smiled,
>
> He stretched out his arms and they encircled the globe.
>
> His vision made giants out of men and organizations.

Mr G D Birla

If J R D Tata had the vision, Mr G D Birla had homely wisdom. His success as India's leading entrepreneur since pre-Partition days is ascribed to his 13 maxims.

- *Jo kal kare so aaj kar.* What you would put off for tomorrow, do today. What you can do today, do now.
- *Dudh ka dudh, paani ka paani.* Learn the art of discrimination.
- *Jo beet gaya so beet gaya.* What is over is the past. Think of the future.
- Time and Tide wait for no one. Similarly opportunities knock only once at your door.
- Every mistake is an experience. If you learn from it, it proves to be a blessing, if you don't, you suffer.
- *Kar bhala, to ho bhala.* Always extend a helping hand.
- *Aram Haram hai.* Hard work never killed anyone.
- Early to bed, early to rise, makes a person healthy, wealthy and wise.
- The hand of the Giver is higher than that of the receiver.
- To err is human, to forgive divine.
- Be humble and speak politely.
- Life is an input-output ratio. It is like a sea of milk. The more you churn it, the more buttermilk you get out of it.
- Knowledge is limitless. If you think you know it all, you know nothing.

An NRI's View

I have been amazed at the young achievers living abroad. When I met globetrotter Kishore, head of a financial company, I was surprised by his passion for work. One thing was obvious. He put in more effort than many other young men of his age. After working for 15 hours a day, he relaxed on alternate weekends with his family. This is what he revealed, when interviewed.

- *Single task – single minded attention*

Single task helps to concentrate on the job hundred per cent. It leaves the mind uncluttered. Clarity of mind is necessary for success. Always finish one task and then take up the next.

- *Gut feeling*

I have this gut feeling for anything I undertake to do. Call it sixth sense, call it intuition. It always works. When I meet a client, I get this gut feeling that the negotiations will be fruitful. Over the years I have come to trust my gut feeling. It has worked wonders for me.

- *High level of energy*

Unless you have a high level of positive energy you cannot succeed in today's world. Luckily I have this great energy, this great force, which keeps me going and 'actualizes my achievement'. No, I do not eat anything special that gives me this energy. I do not take vitamins or stress busters. This volatile energy is inborn. It is God's gift. It literally makes me go places and helps me find a place in the sun." So do not romanticize the moon, it is the sun *shakti* that takes you up the ladder of success.

- *Fair and Just*

You have to be fair and just in all your dealings. You can be a strategist or an analyst, but when it comes to actual dealing with people and business deals, you have to be honest, fair and just or else you lose your credibility. That is the worst thing that can happen to you in business.

- *Achievement motivation*

You have to 'will' your achievement. Determination is another word for it. You should be obsessed with your goal. You have got to be completely involved while working

– call it obsession, stubbornness or motivation. It has to be there for you to succeed.

- *Aggressiveness*

You have to be aggressive in order to achieve your goals. Aggression does not mean fighting with one's clients or bosses. But you have to be aggressive enough to push your point of view, in order to convince your clients, colleagues, and sometimes even the boss! Unless you push your views forward, how can you achieve what you want?

- *Relaxed, free attitude*

Efficiency is linked with a relaxed mind. If you are relaxed, you can communicate better, and push your views more effectively. A little tension is part and parcel of a time bound job. It acts like a tonic. But one cannot perform one's best under anxiety and stress.

- *Hard work*

To achieve anything in your life, you have to work hard. When on a project begin your work day with ten hours, then gradually push it to twelve to fourteen hours...

I would like to quote Dr. Abdul Kalam;

> To dream is not to sleep
> To dream is to lose sleep

So many times we ask ourselves the question: What if I am stuck with a problem? Whenever you are stuck with a problem, first of all relax. Do not worry. Worrying will not solve your problem. Try to find a solution with a calm mind. How?

Solutions can be found through 'an hour' of silence. Sit in silence and relax your body and mind. In silence fresh energy flows in the mind and offers solutions. Silence is positive. It heals, uplifts and rejuvenates. It is 'hibernation' which brings forth all the vital energies required for a 'new self'. Silence is active. That's when your powers of intuition unfold, and you become the recipient of many energies. The great artist Michaelangelo received creative 'flashes' in silence.

There is Always a Solution

There are No Mistakes Only Experiences

How often do we exclaim; "That was a mistake!" That bewildered expression of regret and panic gets replayed through life. Some mistakes we forget, others we don't. The mistakes can be as mundane as forgetting to turn the geyser off or to pick up your passport from the airport counter.

There are umpteen excuses to justify mistakes; absentmindedness, preoccupation, distraction, carelessness, nervousness, etc. However, major decisions like relocation of home or an impulsive resignation letter, can cause much trouble and upheaval and lead to regrets that leave you sad and depressed. Some mistakes are irreversible – then is there room for hope ?

Dada J.P. Vaswani would say, "There are no mistakes only experiences. There are no problems only challenges." Every experience teaches us something in life and inspires retrospection and introspection. The experience is humbling and it makes us wiser. That is, if every mistake is regarded as an experience and not as a source of self-pity or self-condemnation. A close friend had to relocate herself due to unavoidable circumstances. She could not reconcile herself to the change. Every mishap in her life began to seem to her to be the result of her relocation. Stuck in the groove of the blame culture and rooted in her past, she failed to realize the lifetime benefits she had received from this relocation.

Nature abounds in examples of flexibility and relocation in case of birds and animals. Scientific research in the behaviour of birds had confirmed this. Birds and animals travel miles in search of better food, congenial climate and safety. These relocations may no doubt cause some amount of stress, but they are also a source of survival: helping in group bonding and cooperation; and to explore the beauty of a new space and better environment.

"To the weak, problems are stumbling blocks, to the brave, they are stepping stones". An untimely termination letter is certainly traumatic and disturbing. But think of the possibilities it can throw open for you. A young man felt disappointed when he failed in an interview for a corporate job. Looking back he says "It was a blessing in disguise. I would have never reached this far otherwise."

Some mistakes bring out a very important message. Here is a true story. The big boss of a transnational construction company was jubilant at having bagged a major contract. Soon his joy turned into tears when he realized that he had forgotten to include a major component of the cost. What a colossal loss it would bring to the company. He thought for a while and then called one of his colleagues, who he trusted and confided the blunder he had committed. The colleague took up the challenge and worked out a strategy to justify the faith reposed in him.

When the project was complete, it had made a huge profit. The colleague said, "It is the trust placed in me that worked. I called up my contacts, friends and batchmates and eliminated the middle engineering costs. Each one of my fiends helped to cut the costs. I had faith in them. This experience has taught me a great lesson. Trust and faith work. My boss's faith in me, and my faith in my professional buddies together helped us to sail through the troubled waters, to the profit shore."

Dada J.P. Vaswani would say, "Believe and Achieve! And faith is essential in order to do so. It is triple faith that men need today—faith in oneself, faith in the world around us, and above all, faith in God!"

We often worry over the mistakes we make, even those that might have been made unconsciously. The best solution is not always the easiest. This is well illustrated by the story of Leonardo da Vinci. He was working on his (now famous) painting, 'The Last Supper', when he became angry with a certain man and literally hurled abuses at him. Returning to his canvas, he attempted to work on the face of Jesus, but was unable to do so. He was perturbed at his inability to concentrate. Finally he put down his tools and went over to the man he had treated harshly. He asked for forgiveness. The man accepted his apology. Leonardo then felt light at heart and was able to continue painting.

Now we know how to rectify our mistakes and solve corporate and personal problems. *Sometimes the solutions are at hand.* I remember how, Late Mr. Vilas Rao Salunkhe, the great industrialist engineer turned social entrepreneur found a solution to a constant drought in Maharashtra, India in a very simple way. He said, 'The solution was at hand.'

Here is his story

> Maharashtra saw a severe drought in the year 1971-1972. The situation was so bad, that the state government had to launch an Employment Guarantee Scheme as part of relief measures. Witnessing the plight of drought stricken people, a young engineer was so moved, that he vowed to do something for them.
>
> Mr. Vilasrao Salunkhe recounted, "Out for a walk one morning, I saw thousands of men and women sweating under the fierce sun for a few rupees that helped them survive. The whole sight was pathetic, almost inhuman.

I talked to these famished people and discovered to my dismay that out of the population of 1,50,000 people in Purandhar Taluka, 40,000 were engaged in breaking black rocky boulders. What an illogical solution to drought?"

Salunkhe and his wife Kalpana talked to the people and asked them what they would prefer to do, given an alternative? Their answer was surprising. Given an opportunity they would dig percolation tanks and have water for irrigation. Drought had to be fought by water and not by breaking stones.

The couple moved along with their children to Naigaon, and set up 'Gram Gaurav Pratishtan', or the Village Pride Trust. "We lived like villagers in a small one room house," narrates Kalpana, who holds a degree in social work. "At first it was hard on the children, but one has to sacrifice a lot to achieve results at the grass roots. I used a kerosene stove for cooking and we slept on the floor."

For five long years from 1974 onwards the Salunkhes carried out experiments in water and soil conservation; in low-capital cost community irrigation works.

It is here that the concept of Pani Panchayat was born. Panchayat means a council. It is a traditional institution for the management of a village or community. Inspired by the merits of this institution Mr. Salunkhe applied it to the most natural resource needed in agriculture i.e. water.

He said, "Pani Panchayat is a whole meal. It is an integral planning of water system at the micro-level, which takes care of macro problems of afforestation, crop-pattern, agricultural productivity and basic minimum needs." Its effects are numerous. The major effect of Pani Panchayat has been that of reverse migration due to the prosperity of the villages under the system.

Mr Vilasrao Salunkhe's success story is based on the following ideals:
- *Nishkama karma* (selfless action)
- Compassion for humanity
- Service before self
- Application of his scientific knowledge at grass roots
- Austere living
- Faith in God and in human beings
- Training leadership from within
- Family support

Leadership Secrets

A leader is like the captain of a ship. Once a Merchant Navy ship was sailing from Chile to Japan. Due to heavy rains and lashing waves, some water had seeped into the cargo hold. The ship shuddered. The cargo was of logs of wood. The ship was steered towards the nearest coast but with about a hundred miles to go the ship began to tilt on one side. The logs of wood had expanded with the water, and hence had become very heavy. The captain knew the ship was going to sink. He called his crew members and discussed the situation and it was decided to vacate the ship. As per rules, under such situations, the junior most officers leave the first, with the rest following in ascending order of seniority. The captain is the last to leave. One by one the lifesaving boats were lowered and by the time the contingent of crew members left, three fourths of the ship was in water. The captain was left with a wooden plank, a kind of raft, which he threw into the water and then jumped on. The captain of the ship is a true leader!

Have you watched a flock of birds in flight? They do not fly at random. They fly in an inverted V formation, the weakest birds fly at the end while the strongest are in front. The strongest being the leader, plunges into the uncertain air currents in front, creating an upwash that provides better aerodynamics to those behind it. The young and the weak birds at the end of the formation, benefit from the lesser amount of drag created by this and can travel longer distances with lesser fatigue, than they would otherwise have done. If any of the birds is exhausted and cannot fly, the birds in the vanguard accompany it to the ground, protecting it from falling a prey to predatory birds. This is a wonderful lesson in Leadership.

Have you watched the movie 'Lagaan'? To many of us it a throw back to historical times, a slice from life during British rule. But to a student of management it was a lesson in leadership. For Bhuvan (Aamir Khan), the leader of the team, selected his team carefully and motivated it to fight to the finish. This resulted in a great victory.

Sharing secrets

Anil Singhvi of Reliance Natural Resources Ltd (RNRL) began his career as an ordinary employee and rose to be the Vice Chairman of the company. Sharing his experiences with the students of FLAME, he said, "Leadership largely embodies passion. Look for simple answers even to complex problems. You have to love what you are doing."

Seventy six per cent of people who fail to fulfil their life and dreams, do so because of deficiencies in their personality. These deficiencies can be corrected.

For this the **first step** is to *accept* the deficiencies in one's personality.

The **second step** is to take the advice of proficient people as to how to correct them. The **third step** is to actually remove the deficiencies, miracles will not happen. There is no magic wand or spell that will materialize golden eggs from thin air. But, if we seek the help of wisdom of God, miracles can become our everyday experience.

The nature of our existence is such that we cannot function effectively unless we have faith. This is the secret spiritual law of life. This faith has to be cultivated diligently. It becomes strong when we understand the perfection in the functioning of the Universe—the tremendous forces which make the clouds rain, the grass grow; trees to bear fruit and the tides to rise and ebb. The force behind all this is also the force behind our success.

The second secret spiritual law of success is – sow a seed and reap a tree. For whatever you give of yourself, you make way for the Return of Gratitude by Nature itself.

On the one hand we overcome self deficiencies and on the other we follow the secret laws. And Lo and behold! Success is ours.

New Horizons, New Stars

N R Narayana Murthy, the chairman and CEO of Infosys has this statement to make, "It is leaders who raise aspirations. It is leaders who raise the confidence of people. It is leaders who make people say, 'We'll walk on water.' So the importance of leadership for the good of the company can never be exaggerated."

Who is a leader?
- The one who has nobility of mind
- The one who has wisdom
- The one who can sacrifice for his team/followers
- The one who wants to give his co-workers the Best in the world
- The one who inspires and endures the risks

> *Emotion is the key to success. Emotions are the key that generate required enthusiasm for performance of duties towards others from others' reasonable point of view with a strong and sharp sense of duty. Such emotional involvement towards the organization in day-to-day work properly balances out the quality, cost and time demands which give the desired productivity.*
>
> **Subrata Roy, *Guardian of Sahara family***

Emotional Quotient is not a new term. Many company heads go by the gut/ emotion/feeling. Being emotional does not mean being irrational or devoid of reason. In fact it means being more reasonable, fair and just. It means being more involved. Emotion is strength.

Kevin Tan's workplace philosophy, *'Keep going, or else, the rest may just catch up with you"* implies that you should follow knowledge beyond the utmost bounds of human thought. Keep upgrading.

Azim Premji, Chairman of Wipro, said at the Symbiosis Institute of Management and Mass Communication, "what we had is a set of values which we cherished. They have stood us in good stead and have been the backbone of our organization. Values reduce transaction costs, get you better employees, customers and better business."

A leaf from the diary of a President of a business association written in 1936:

- Begin the day with a five minute silence. A man ought always to be reminded to pray to God in his own way and according to his own spirit.
- To be faithful to one another and to those we serve.
- To develop the character, ability, success, and security of every co-worker.
- To create a personality that will be known for its strengths and friendliness.
- To build a business that will never know completion, but that will always step forward to meet advancing conditions.
- To take part in building a finer, better community in which to live.

> *Thermax believes in nurturing a human organization which understands the paradox that the total organization is more important than the individual but this does not make the individual less important.*
>
> **The Late Rohinton D Aga,**
> **Managing Director, Thermax**

Anu Aga, chairman of Thermax, a Rs 500 crore engineering unit, states that, "To be a good leader, one must be able to lay enormous faith in people and their ability to make a difference. The key to success in business is treating people with respect and allowing them to perform to their fullest. What is success? Success is not about winning at work and losing at life. The bottom line is being a good sensitive individual."

Padamshree Leela Poonawala says, "I have ten commandments for success:

- *To have the ability to strategise whatever you do*
- *Tactfully be forceful*
- *You must have a dream or a vision*
- *Inspiration followed by persuasion. Lead from the front*
- *You should have courage and guts*
- *Delegation of authority is a must*
- *Effective communication, which means listening with attention*
- *Negotiations*
- *Attention to detail*

The Challenge of Changing the Mindset

Our cultural conditioning determines our attitudes. In a country like India which has a rigid normative system, the easiest way to survive psychologically is through escapism. Every failure, personal or otherwise, is attributed to another person. In other words, we practice what the corporate sociologists call blame culture or passing the buck.

If we fail to make the grade in the academic field we blame it on the teaching faculty or non-availability of library books or the grading modalities of the examination system. If we fail to make the grade in our career, we blame the boss or the organization or sometimes the domestic conditions. We never own up responsibility for our failure.

According to Singapore based Shatrughan Yadav, Managing Director, Go Mad Pvt Ltd., "Successful people have a very strong sense and measure of personal responsibility. When outcomes are favourable we take credit for our smart moves, even if they merely involved swinging a pendulum! When outcomes do not turn out the way we want them to, we should still take responsibility and not blame astrologers, tarot cards or the coin."

In India the failure of politicians and film stars is often blamed on the astrologer for prescribing the wrong stones, dates and constituencies.

A shift in mindset is necessary here. For instance, instead of blaming we should change to:

a) Analysis of the failure;
b) The choices available;
c) Marking the learning route (every failure teaches a lesson)
d) Taking action to remedy the situation

In today's dynamic world we should shrug off the old negative culture and move on to the new positive culture of responsibility. The term responsibility should not mean burdensome duty. It is an active reaction or a response to an event or a situation. The secret to success is simple – change the mindset. Loosen the ties of negative norms. Internalize the following success formula:

- There are no mistakes in life, only experiences
- Every experience is a learning route to success
- There are no failures – only opportunities. Your success lies in how quickly you can grab them
- There are no hurdles – only choices. Make the right choice for the great miracle to happen .
- There are no blame guinea pigs – only responsibility. Empower yourself to practice it the right way.

Success Through The Power Within

We are ignorant of the power within. Each one of us has an Infinite source of power; call it soul, spirit, or light. We have only to tap it. Once this power is opened and used, it works miracles. This power is hidden is wrapped by negative emotions like hate, jealousy, envy, greed and selfishness. Discard these negative feelings, and the power within flows like an unending stream.

That one call

Recently at a seminar on business success, held in Pune, Arun Nathani, CEO &M.D. CYBAGE INDIA recounted his entrepreneurial adventure. Therein he narrated how at a point during the phase of negotiation, he was stuck. That is when he tapped this Infinite source for help to tide over the hurdle.

He had applied for a particular project to a USA based company. As in such cases, anxiety mounted, as there was a long delay in receiving the reply. Then the call came; but he was in Chicago, and his interview was in San Francisco. He hurriedly dashed to San Francisco, taking the night flight. He reached just in time to present himself for the interview. During the interview it became clear, that the project could successfully take off in India, if he were given the assistance of four engineers from the organization. The sanction for this had to come from the head office and that was the hitch. He waited for that important call, and when nothing seemed to be happening, he appealed to the great POWERS above.

'You got to help me,' he said. And the help came. The call came and negotiations were successfully completed. The Higher Powers or that power within resolved the deadlock. Starting with three engineers, and him, Arun Nathani today has more than three thousand technically qualified staff and his company, CYBAGE INDIA, founded in 1995, is a Global Offshore Software Services Company. It is ranked in the 2009 'GLOBAL SERVICES 100' list. It is one of the most successful IT industries, in the world.

Needless to say that Arun Nathani had all his equations right—his negotiating skill, his analytical vision, and his marketing strategies—but for the success, it was that small request-'YOU GOT TO HELP ME,' that ultimately kicked the engine to start.

To tap that inner power, two things are necessary – **one** to purify oneself through harnessing love, unconditional, for all, and **two**, a bit of meditation, to connect with that power within.

Angels In The Backyard

Dr. Ragunath Anant Mashelkar went barefoot to school. He had to walk five miles to the school every day, because there was none in his village. He had no books to study from, no electricity at home. He borrowed books, copied them, and literally read them under the old hurricane lamp. The dire circumstances nearly compelled him to give up studies, even though he was a rank holder at the matriculation examination. An advertisement in the newspaper, offering scholarship to the deserving and needy students drew the attention of his teacher, who encouraged him to apply for it. By luck Ragunath was selected but had to present himself at the head office of the Tata Education Trust, in Bombay.

Ragunath travelled by bus to Bombay, and by the time he reached the office, he looked a real rustic bump. He entered the office and was awed by its sophistication. He was served tea in the typical English style and he did not know how to make it. The kind Parsee lady behind the reception counter helped him. She taught him how to make the tea English style and use forks and spoon. In fact till that day he had not seen a fork or a tea kettle. That Parsee lady turned out to be his guardian Angel at every step. The rest is a fairy tale.

Ragunath completed his Ph.D. in Chemical Engineering, in the year 1969. Today Dr. Mashelkar is the president of the Global Research Alliance. So far he has been awarded 26 PhDs, from prestigious universities all over the world. For several years he was the Director of C S I R, and even as of now represents several international organizations.

What made this poor rustic boy reach the top of the scientific world?

The Will To Succeed! At a recent event held by the Weikfield Foundation which gives scholarships to deserving science students from the rural area, Dr. Mashelkar, narrated his journey to the top. Never Be Defeated; Never Be Low. Meet the challenges of life with passion, and fervour, and sure enough you will be the winner. And whatever you achieve is your own merit.'

Dr. Mashelkar has proved the formula of success – Potential +Passion+ Perseverance.

His angels notwithstanding, Dr. Mashelkar's success is due to his strong mind and the will to make it Big.

Inner Strength

Often success in career is associated with education in prestigious foreign universities like Harvard and Stanford. But that need not be so. Chanda Kochar, CEO and MD, ICICI Bank, who is ranked among the twenty most powerful women in the world, by Forbes Magazine, 2009, is a home grown specie. In fact when she was offered a seat at the IIM, Ahmedabad, she chose to be at home in Bombay, and joined Jamnalal Bajaj Institute of Business Management.

Chanda Kochar learnt her lessons early in life, when her father passed away. Right from her early childhood her mother gave her strong middle class values which have stood her in good stead in her career with ICICI Bank.

The values are:

1. Don't accept negativism; always look at the positive side of things
2. Be content no matter what the circumstances
3. Be humble, think of those below you and not of those above you. Do not pamper your ego.

Chanda Kochar is *Shakti* incarnate. She is a tough decision maker. When asked to name three values in her life which have led her to the top position, her answer was: the **first value** is try to excel in whatever you do. The **second value** is that there is no shortcut for sure, only hard work, hard work, and hard work. The **third value** is having a balanced mind that can balance aggressiveness and calmness. Certain situations require aggressive talk, and certain situations need a calm and composed mind to solve problems.

In her personal life, Chanda Kochar is a simple relaxed person. She balances work and domestic responsibilities beautifully. She is a devoted wife, a loving mother and a wonderful daughter.

Guidelines for Success

Call up your inner strength. By calling on those wonderful inner forces of yours, you "Unlimit" yourself. Your vision becomes broader. Your purpose becomes stronger, your energy becomes greater and you aim higher and live deeper. This awareness comes easily when the mind is uncluttered. In a free mind, the creative power manifests itself beautifully.

One way to declutter your mind is to say no to 'worry' and 'No, Thank you', to vague thoughts that float aimlessly in your mind.

Once you become aware of the 'abundance' of creative power within, you realize that nothing is impossible. Once you are sure that the power within you—the great inner force—will come to your aid, you will aim higher and attempt more.

The 'inner force' is the true wealth you have and which you can cash anytime, anywhere. Through realizing the great amount of wealth you have within, you will never feel afraid of the 'unknown future'. It is this power which gives you real courage and confidence in life.

Be bold, be confident

The experience of the vast energy within you should make you feel confident. Mere dreaming of big or great things is not enough. The 'dream' should be backed by confidence in self and in the people around you. If you do not think big and feel confident about it, be sure you will never move forward. A writer says, "Each one of us is born great; only we do not allow greatness to come near us. Don't sell yourself short; this is easily done if you have little or no faith in yourself. Do not underestimate your value as a person."

Your goals should be well defined

What do you want to achieve? Are you clear about your targets? If you dream of becoming a 'leader', define leadership. To get a clear picture, take a piece of paper and write out in no uncertain terms what type of leadership you wish to acquire; political, corporate, educational, media etc. Once you have a clear picture of the goal, you can take steps towards achieving it.

Action is the name of the game

Dreams will crumble to ashes if efforts are not made to turn them into reality. If you have dreamt of a house, and are confident that the Great Universal Power will help you, then sit down and write the requirements of such a dream: an architect, a contractor, a real estate agent, a banker to finance and so on. Do not halt at the thought stage. Move forward seeking the help of the great Power at every step. The dream house will be ready much before you would have anticipated it.

In short for success you need **IAA** *– Inspiration, Aspiration and Application*

Where does inspiration come from?

"Man has an inborn capacity to be inspired." He should be open to listen to the subtle flow of new ideas which float in during relaxation, in meditation and in linkage with the universe. In silence great things are conceived, and in the 'silent hour' you receive your message of inspiration. Of course your inspiration, mundane or otherwise, will come only when you are willing to listen to your inner voice or to your own heartbeats. Otherwise it will just bypass you.

After receiving an inspiration you should think about it. Then ask yourself, "How can I best use this gift of an idea to my benefit?"

All the great scientists and inventors were inspired by an idea that flashed through their mind in a state of relaxation. Through hard work and perseverance they converted that 'seed' into a tree; an idea into reality. The precious seed is given, not to be thrown away, but to worked upon, especially since it is the idea the universe has given to you.

This requires application, which is really the most difficult task.

The bottom line is; **Believe And Achieve**

The Inner Scape

Creative Visualization And The Poem Of The Mind

Imagine your goal is achieved. Experience it. Feel as if it has happened. The mind, its imagination, its ability to convert a thought into actual reality is great. Swami Vivekananda in his speech delivered at Los Angeles, California on January 8, 1900 tells us about the extraordinary happenings, which are nothing but the 'actualization' of a powerful mind. Swamiji once went to such a man to test his powers. I quote, "He wrote something on paper, which he folded up, asked me to sign at the back and said, 'Don't look at it, put it in your pocket and keep it there till I ask for it again. After a while he said, 'Now, think of a word or sentence, from any language you like.' I thought of a long sentence from Sanskrit, a language of which he was entirely ignorant. 'Now take out the paper from your pocket' he said. The Sanskrit sentence was written there! He had written it an hour before with the remarks, 'In confirmation of what I have written, this man will think of this sentence'."

A hundred years ago this seemed awesome, extraordinary and miraculous. Today it is scientific and commonplace knowledge.

Actualization of thought occurs when:

- The intensity of thought is great
- When the thought is solidified by enunciating it in writing
- By reaffirming it with positivism

- This is to be done when the mind is absolutely relaxed, and
- In tune with its source, the cosmic Intelligence

Human beings possess extraordinary powers of mind. The human mind is a part of the universal mind. It is linked with the universal mind and can achieve everything under the sun. We have to learn to tap this knowledge; the power of the mind. How can we develop Mind power?

The individual's power of thought has long been recognized. Even before the birth of Jesus Christ, Manlius, a famous Roman wrote, "No barriers, no masses, however enormous, can withstand the powers of the mind. The remotest corners yield to them, all things succumb, and the very heaven itself is laid open." This power of thought builds up confidence.

Lateral thinking

Have you read *Zen and the Art of Motorcycle Repair*? Read it. Learn the art of lateral thinking. Lateral thinking means offbeat thinking. There is a phrase in Hindi, *"Zara Hatke,"* which literally means, off the beaten track. Thinking out of the box can bring about unusual solutions; or even creative solutions, which are extremely helpful.

Lateral thinking is akin to a brainstorming session of executives in the corporate world. For instance, making work seem more attractive, like Tom Sawyer did. Tom makes a tedious job like whitewashing, attractive by using his wit. What was drudgery became sheer fun. Well, this is lateral thinking in the area of delegation. You tempt others into doing tedious unpleasant jobs by making them look attractive and rewarding.

I have loved Kahlil Gibran's story, which I would like to share with you. For it is all about looking ahead, having a vision. There cannot be success without a vision!

Vision Beyond

Kahlil Gibran has beautifully portrayed the concept of 'A Vision Beyond', in a short story. The story goes something like this:

> *A fragrant and beautiful violet in a garden with roses complained – 'How unfortunate am I! How humble is the position I occupy. Look at the rose. It is tall and looks up to the sky. I live very close to the earth and I cannot raise my head towards the blue sky or to the sun. The tall rose heard this and said, 'You are fortunate. Nature has bestowed upon yourself the fragrance and beauty, which she did not grant to any other flower. Remember, that he who humbles himself will be exalted and he who exalts himself will be humbled and crushed.' Nature heard their conversation, and said to the Violet, "What has happened to you my daughter Violet? You have always been humble." The Violet answered, "O Merciful mother grant me a request. Allow me to be a rose for one day." To which Nature answered, 'You know not what you are seeking. You are unaware of the concealed disaster behind your blind ambition. Nevertheless, the Violet insisted and the Merciful Mother Nature obliged. The Violet became a tall handsome rose. In the evening, the sky became thick with black clouds. The thunder tore the sky into sheets of rain and ruined the garden. All the flowers lay scattered except the violets clutching on to the earth. The queen of violets was happy and she told her Violet family, "We are small, and live close to the earth, but we are spared the wrath of the sky. Look at the Violet that became a rose for day."*
>
> *The dying rose, looked up and said, "I am happy now because I have probed outside my little world into the mystery of the Universe. I listened to the silence of the Night and I heard 'Ambition beyond existence is the essential purpose of our being'.*

> *I have realized that purpose. I have looked at the Universe from behind the eyes of the rose. I have extended my knowledge to a world beyond the narrow cavern of my birth. This is the design of life. This is the secret of existence, "Yes one has to look beyond, and experience things outside of one's everyday existence. One has to dream and be ambitious to go that far.*

Jawaharlal Nehru has said, "Low ambition, not failure, is crime."

So aim high.

If you have the will to go beyond, you will.

Think BIG!

Man is what he thinks. As it is said, Energy follows Thoughts. When you think big, you are motivated to achieve it.

Disappointed? Bounce Back

A friend of mine appeared for an interview at a world renowned auto company for the post of senior executive. The interview went off well. He was sure of getting the coveted job, because his training and qualifications matched the job requirement. As luck would have it, he was rejected outright. *How did he react to this big disappointment?*

It was a setback, more so as he had planned to move with his family and worked out the details of it, like fixing the house, and children's admissions. Being pragmatic he did not give up so easily. He did not sit and brood over the why he was rejected, or why his abilities did not impress the board of interviewers.

He sought out similar companies and applied for the same post in those companies. The rejection spurred him on, and he utilized it as a learning process. He even used the interview as a spring board for his future interviews. Within a year he succeeded in bagging a prestigious job in a global concern, with a much higher remuneration than he would have got in the first interview. He had turned his disappointment into the perseverance and determination to succeed.

> *You have to just keep in mind that a setback is only temporary and greater things lie ahead. Believe in the two steps forward, one step back philosophy.*
> **Shriram Shinde,** *journalist and wildlife writer*

Perseverance Pays

Edmund Hillary was not the first one to try to scale Mt. Everest. There were a few before him who had almost reached the peak but fell a victim to inclement weather, deadly blizzards, and blinding snowstorms. That did not deter him from scaling the heights and conquering the peak.

"We did not know if it was humanly possible to reach the Mt. Everest. And even using oxygen, if we did not get to the top, we weren't at all sure whether we wouldn't drop dead or something of that nature," is what Edmund Hillary said after conquering the world's greatest peak. Knowing that it might be impossible, he yet attempted to do what others feared, more so because of the number of climbers disappearing into the blizzards around the peak. One of these climbers had attempted fifty four times, and when he was almost there, he fell down into the snow bound valley, dead and buried for over half a century in that snowy tomb. Nothing deterred Edmund Hillary from his goal.

J K Rowling faced 16 rejections for her first book, *Harry Potter and the Philosopher's Stone*. In fact the book was rejected by publishers so many times that she decided to publish it herself. She lived like an average commoner in a small house in England. She was disappointed with the rejection slips, but she turned the corner by turning them into fresh appointments with new publishers. Rowling looked at different options available in publishing her works.

Today Rowling enjoys worldwide success. Her books are being turned into movies. Children adore her writing and crave for more. If Rowling had stopped at the 15th publisher she would have missed the phenomenal success enjoyed by her now.

It is said of Ernest Hemingway, that his book *The Old Man and the Sea*, which is considered a masterpiece, was revised nearly a hundred times, before it got published.

> Approach life with perseverance and dedication To do the things that matter most to you. Success is never easy. It remains up to you whether you will give up or fight through the tough battle to earn whatever it is you want.
>
> **Shriram Shinde (*Big Leap*)**

Make your goals achievable.

The latest mantra doing rounds of HRD courses is a phrase from *Gurbani*: *Sahaj Subah Jo Hoe So Ho*. It means, 'Whatever happens naturally is the best.' This mantra is considered to be the best antidote today. The Sikh Guru who coined this phrase could foresee the momentum of life and the tumult of tensions and the ensuing frustrations. Tensions more often than not give way to frustration. Frustration is the major cause of unhappiness and most of us find it difficult to cope up with daily frustrations.

Very often we pursue goals and desires which are unrealistic, as unrealistic as shadows. We pursue them with faith and determination hoping that persistence will yield results. This is not bad at all. But when the goal seems far and unreachable we should not bang our head against the iron wall and bleed. According to Osho, "No matter what you do, life turns out the way it turns out. Struggling with life does not help at all."

In pursuing our goals and desires we encounter delays, blockages and obstructions. That is when we throw up our hands in frustration and wonder, "Why can't I do it?" and determine to fulfil our dreams come what may. This may be a healthy attitude but it should not push us to a wall, which we can neither climb nor break. In such a case it is best to stop and give it a rest.

Take time off from your obsession. Create a relaxed space within yourself. For on this journey there are waiting rooms, transit lounges, and pit stops. Make use of them. The truth is that Time, Trust, and Tryst must synchronize to yield fulfilment. By that time you may discover a new purpose, goal, or even a new obsession!

Success Mantra From Movies

To many who watched the movie 'Nautch' it was a disaster—long, boring and repetitive. But management students differ in their views. The movie carries at least three messages for success: perseverance, crossing umpteen hurdles, and the passion for the goal/purpose. In all it teaches us not to give up when we are convinced of our ideology and ability to put it into practice.

'Lagaan' is another painfully dull movie. But it is a lesson in management. The village team defeats the sophisticated players of the British in a game of cricket. The success is due to the choice of the members of the team. The leader Bhuvan, selects the team judiciously and designates an appropriate role to each member.

A good leader chooses his team taking into account its qualities and abilities for a particular job. A leader cannot achieve anything alone. It is the team work that leads to success. In a team each member is as important as the other, suitable for his job and hence can give his best to it. The leader is the director, the team members are the real actors, and together they make success possible. Right person for the job spells success. As the management proverb goes: Avoid a round peg in a square hole.

Seven Novel Ways to Shoo Away those Executive Anxieties

"We are all running for three meals a day", wails a Marathi poet. We may add, that if not for three meals a day, for more cheese and cake. But we all are in the rat race, running faster every day. So fast indeed that at forty, most executives are literally out of breath. Says an executive turned ascetic, "I'm looking forward to my retirement; I want to be away from this cut-throat competition. I can't last for more than a few years, in this stifling environment."

This desire for escapism is the outcome of 'thirty-forty stress'. The period when work becomes an obsession, the centre of the universe, with those workaholic refrains – "I have no time for anything, haven't watched a movie, been on a holiday. Just cannot afford all that. I have to make the grade. If I don't make it now, I shall never be able to make it."

The common fallacy that your potential gets best expression between thirty-forty has robbed many of the best years of their life. The stress devastates all the finer things of life. (What Burce calls 'unsought graces of life') One misses the fun of playing with a child and of spending time with one's better half, family or friends.

It is not before long that the frenzy of forty develops into frustration, for there isn't enough room at the top. All institutions, corporations, and establishments are pyramidal.

It is interesting to come across the, "I am hurt, you are hurt" dialogue at the executive desk. The typical dialogues run somewhat like this: "Behind every financially successful man is a sleazy past. Believe me, it is cent per cent true." or "To reach the top you don't have to climb up, you have to be pulled up."; or "If I had a bit of luck on my side, I would have shown them. We are professionals, we are technocrats, and they are money riders. Have a look at the tops and see who all are perched there? Hawks!" Of course this kind of situation is more common in organizations that are family managed.

A friend at the top of professional hierarchy says, "Everyday I enter the office with a depressed feeling. I get the feeling they are all waiting for me to leave, so that one of them can grab my chair. And you have to be cautious of them all the time, for you never know who will knife you in the back." This tug-of-war played out at the top in many organizations is evidence of the power politics, ego-clashes and leadership whipping. What else can you expect in a society where success is synonymous with top job actualization? Perhaps it is working under these conditions that causes career hazards, which harden the arteries of the heart and line the stomach with ulcers; freezes the brain with fear. The fear neurosis, under which most of us work, requires more than mere psychiatric treatment. It requires correction of the adverse demand and supply equation in the employment market; correction of the power structure and redistribution of authority. All these are macro problems outside the scope of an individual.

Despair always gives vent to philosophy. It is necessary to have a philosophy of work in order to survive, because out of an average lifespan of seventy years, forty years are spent in earning a living, and twenty before that in preparing to earn it. Let us see how people arrive at conclusions. Mr. K. thirty, and middle level executive, "Job is not everything. There is something larger and bigger – the job is only one of the things in life. If you can't make it to the top, it's O.K."

THE SECRET ROUTE

Discovering the Route

Great men like Albert Einstein, Mahatma Gandhi, and Albert Schweitzer knew the secret route to success. The secret route has been revealed by the great scriptures of the world. A Sikh bhajan goes: *Jo mange thakur se apna yahan wahain hoe.* Meaning, whatever you ask of God is already there. Further, whatever you ask of God is granted.

The Bible has it too. 'Ask and it will be given to you, seek and you shall find, knock the door and it shall be opened to you.'

I think it is again in the sacred scriptures of the Sikhs, *Kya nahin ghar tere, mere sai, jis dive, so pave.*' What is it that you cannot give? Whomsoever you give, receives it .

Recently the western world has woken up to the ancient Indian belief , 'ask and it shall be granted.'

How?

When we go to the Echo point in Mahableshwar our voice returns as an echo. In the same way Nature does not keep anything with itself. Whatever you give is returnes out of its goodness. One of the fundamental laws of Nature is 'Nature's response'. It is now scientifically proven that trees, plants, animals and flowers, emotionally respond to human love and care. If you ask Nature to help you, it will.

How? You may ask. For this you have to know the technique of getting your requests accepted.

First, be relaxed. Practice any simple method of relaxation. Second, try and build a relationship with Nature. Third, purify your mind by driving out the devil of negativism. Fourth, sit in silence. Light a lamp. Concentrate on it. Then pray to the Universe and put in your request. Do it several times.

One of the greatest Laws of this Universe is acknowledgement. The Universe is bound to acknowledge your request as truth. And your wish is fulfilled, goal is reached.

Remember you have to search and find the secret route and you have to go through that route. Heavens aren't going to oblige without your efforts. For as you sow, so shall you reap.

More About The Route

It is a well known fact that Nature abhors vacuum. Nature is creative and fills the Universe with its energy and activity. Dr. Jayant Narlikar, the world renowned scientist has said, 'There is tremendous energy around us, which is invisible to the Naked eye.' This energy is not idle but works constantly. For example, when we sow a seed, and nourish it with water, and sunlight, it gives birth to a beautiful flower. It is simply the work of energy in the Universe.

'Believe me', says Nikhil, the universal HRS Guru, 'Every moment of life is infinitely creative and the Universe is endlessly bountiful.' Just put forth a clear 'request' and everything your heart desires will come true. It may take time. Just as in Nature, an apple tree bears fruit after twenty years, the result of your efforts may take a long time to materialize, but they will.

For the subtle law of the universe is as accurate as the physical law of input–output, or the law that "every action has an equal and opposite reaction" or that "energy is never destroyed, it is converted". The subtle laws of the universe work in a very simple way. When the energy of the 'deepest desire' mingles with the energy of the universe, which is divine, then things just happen. Every 'request' we send out to the universe/nature is answered. If help is asked for, help is given; if good health is asked for, good health is given; if peace is asked for, peace is given. Remember, Nature responds with the same strength with which your 'request' is sent. Greater the mental relaxation, greater the strength of your request, higher the possibility of response. We should understand that nature is only a vehicle, the route is the universal quotient, and the destination is success. The universal quotient in simple language means linking the cosmic power and one's own mental power. This secret route was known to our Rishis, as it has now become known to present day psycho spiritualists.

God's image of success for you is always greater than your own. To help it manifest, declare: "The Divine image of success now manifests for me."

Then let it work. Sometimes it may work totally differently. But believe that God's image of success for you is complete and satisfying.

In each one of us lies tremendous *shakti*, call it spiritual strength/power. Once this *Shakti* is awakened you can fly from peak to peak. The spiritual quotient is a matter of 3Fs:
- Fearlessness – Freedom from mental and physical fears
- Faith – Faith either in oneself, or in the Almighty
- Focus – A fixed goal to which one's energies should be directed

Work effortlessly

- *Live each day as it comes*

"Finish each day and be done with it. You have done what you could. Some blunders and absurdities have crept in. Forget them as soon as you can."

Ralph Waldo Emerson

- *Build Check dams*

Check dams stop the overflow of mental tension. Build a check dam of diversions. Stop mental hurry. Hurry will only cause you worry. Every time there is a rush of jobs to be done take a break: you may try this simple exercise – count ten backwards, take ten deep breaths and relax.

- *Make a list of jobs to be done*

Make a list of jobs to be done according to their priorities. You will realise that half the anxiety is about those jobs which can be easily done or can be dismissed within minutes. Some of the anxiety is the result of the replay of thoughts/incidents/actions and is a total waste of mental energy.

- *Repeat the mantra*

Tensions/Anxiety are caused by diffidence. Reinforce positivism. Repeat the 'I am successful' mantra twenty times just before falling off to sleep at night. Do so, first thing in the morning too.

- *Get up on the right side of the bed*

Well that is an old saying, but not without meaning. A simple test of whether you are getting up on the right or the wrong side is to check whether your breath is exhaled through the left nostril. If you exhale through the left nostril then put your right foot down first, it has to do with the body rhythm alignment. The right nostril represents positivism; the left, negativism. The idea is to get up with a positive thought.

- *Build a holiday resort within*

Learn to have a space within where you can enter for rejuvenation: a space of tranquillity, peace and, bliss. Build the holiday resort step by step; make it your hideout.

Discovering the Route

Visit your recovery room everyday
Recharge your energy with prayer. A few minutes of silence and a few minutes of recollecting good memories, incidents, and a few minutes of thanks giving can fill your mind with the joy of positivism.

Make every task not a compulsion but a pleasure

Certainty in an uncertain world
The financial tsunami of 2008 left many shattered. The 26/11 bomb blasts in Bombay traumatized the world. The dark clouds of terrorism hang low over the globe. Violence has become an active volcano, its' molten lava turns things and people into ashes. Insecurity and uncertainty has gripped mankind as never before. There is need for Peace and Prayer.

What is a prayer?
It was a beautiful sunset. The dusk had gathered the colours of the Gulmohar into its folds. The sky was suffused with a scarlet red. Temple bells chimed in the distance. In that mystical hour of metamorphosis, silence whispered. That whisper was a prayer. It attuned me to the mystery of nature.

A prayer is an elevating experience of wonder. It is not words, it is a feeling. This feeling can be experienced anywhere and everywhere. Truly, it is said, 'Prayer is the wisdom of the heart and purity of mind.'

Normally we associate prayer with worship or rituals. It is selfish as it is loaded with *quid pro quo*. Most of our prayers are contract deals or barter programs. We keep asking God for this or that. But god is not a candy slot machine where you insert your prayer currency and obtain the candy of your heart's desire.

Prayer is like love; unconditional; an outpouring of feeling of the soul. It is giving, and not taking.

Christina Rosetti says in her poem,

> In the bleak mid-winter
> Frosty wind made moan,
> Earth stood hard as iron,
> Water, like a stone.
> If I were a wise man
> I would do my part –
> Yet what can I give Him;
> Give my heart!

Prayer, even as an abstract feeling has many dressing gowns. To the young it is an online chat with the Cosmic Intelligence, to the old it is a tete-e-tete with the Supreme self, to others it is a poem to the almighty or the Cosmic power. In whichever way you look at it prayer is a pure positive energy. It gives one strength derived from the influence of the spirit.

Why do we pray? Overtly we pray for a variety of reasons, but in reality, they all converge in one word, "Peace." Peace too has many dimensions and myriad meanings. To know the true meaning of peace, here is an interesting ancient story. Once upon a time there was a king. He announced a grand prize for the artist who would paint the best picture of 'Peace'.

Artists from far and near participated in the event and several paintings depicting 'peace' were presented to the king. Of these he chose only two. The first painting showed a calm serene lake surrounded by lofty mountains, their reflections, mystical. The azure blue sky peppered with fluffy clouds. The second picture showed thunder and lightening in an angry sky. Its mountains were bare except for a gushing waterfall. This painting was vibrant, energetic, but very ordinary. The king chose the second painting even though the first had won the popular vote. Why? Because that painting showed a bush in a niche in the rugged mountain by the side of the waterfall. A mother bird had built her nest in it. A quiet amidst the thunder and turbulence of nature. That is the real meaning of peace. It's for this 'peace' that we pray.

Most of us find it difficult to recite 'verses' *'gathas'* or 'mantra'. Most of us find it difficult to sit in one place in silence. Prayer, even as a feeling has different brands.

Serving the poor is a prayer. Meditation is prayer. Reflecting or reflections in water and shadows playing on the earth is also meditation. Viewing oneself in the mirror from the sky is prayer.

That is why many saints in the west have said, 'Any good thoughts expressed with the heart, is a prayer." To put it differently, 'thinking in the presence of god is a nutrient to our soul." That's what prayer does.

Prayer is divine experience, free of time, space, and words.

Sadhu T.L. Vaswani has given a beautiful pictorial description of prayer. "Prayer setting up waves in the ether of Spirit, the waves ultimately describing a circle and coming back to you as added *Shakti* and illumination in the measure of the purity and aspiration. True prayer is inner attitude."

It is the inner attitude that transforms us and brings the tranquillity of mind. The source of tranquillity is the security which prayer provides. Sadhu T.L. Vaswani has written, "Prayer is *Shakti*. Prayer is protective power; prayer creates forms which become the guardians of those we pray for, prayer too promotes renovation of life. Prayer checks the wearing of life's forces. Prayer links with the eternal heart." Therefore, it brings peace.

A Resort Within The Mind, All Your Own

Caught up in a sea of turbulence? Stressed out? Want to breathe fresh air and be as light as a feather; to smell the flowers and touch the stars in the sky? Well, you will have to learn some tricks.

One of the tricks is to create a holiday resort all your own: a space in the mind, the heart, the psyche; which would be an oasis of peace; a lake of love, a forest of beauty. A perfect holiday resort, where the snow capped mountains inspire you with their loftiness, the calm rivers wash away your tensions, and the forest of huge trees aligns you with the Spirit of Nature. And the strength of equilibrium, power of positivism, and oneness with the great mystery are all yours.

True, such a holiday resort cannot be created in a day. It requires years of effort, positive thoughts, erasing one's ego and wiping off one's past (history, geography and psychology i.e. of only the unpleasant parts). It is a gigantic task; it will need support of your near and dear ones, of books and booklets, of pilgrimages to energy fields, and faith. Once your holiday resort is ready, you can rest in peace. Whenever there is mental turmoil, a tense situation on the personal front, or everyday stress building up, all that you have to do is to turn inwards and bathe in the beauty of the forest, or share the waters of love, or simply let your hair down in your 'inner niche' and be relaxed. The holiday resort is the inner space of tranquillity unruffled by the exterior life. It is built in bliss that every individual can carry within him.

How does one really start building one's holiday resort? Slowly, gradually, step by step.

The First step

Apply the rule of a five minute holiday everyday. Take a mental flight to the most beautiful landscape you can remember. Relive it. Relish it. A space for a holiday has been created in your mind/psyche. Being subject to the law of increasing returns, the more such flights you take, the more peaceful you become.

The Second step

A minute long prayer everyday will sow the seeds of faith. In due course faith will bloom and flourish covering the mind's space with flowers of light and fruits of good deeds. It will bear blossoms of bliss. Choose a prayer which is an 'experience' to you. It will act like a rain shower which would wash away the cobwebs of dusty years. For some it is the Gayatri Mantra, for some it is *Soham*, for yet others, 'Our father in heaven' or 'Abide with me'.

The Third step

A three minute meditation everyday will show you the inward journey, the route which passes through the holiday resort. A three minute meditation? Yes, three minutes are sufficient to unload the mental stress and bring relief to the 'core' self. What kind of meditation? The simplest one. The one that makes you surrender everything to the Higher Power and helps you accept everything as the 'Best' solution and the 'Perfect Order': meditation on breath, *Isht Dev*, space, the third eye, or mere Silence. This gets rid of all the mental garbage. All the foul smell escapes with a hiss; allow it to escape.

The Fourth step

Align yourself with nature just for a minute. It is that link road to your holiday resort which brings equanimity, peace, and harmony—an excellent flyover to your destination.
How does one align with Nature? Whisper to a plant, embrace a tree, speak to the stars, sing to the sun and enjoy their company.

The Fifth step

Create a happy memory album. Recollecting one good incident or one happy moment of life everyday will make a good collection of happy moments. If and when you are

Discovering the Route

bored at the Holiday resort you can go through your memory album and feel refreshed. The happy memory album is not escapism; it is more an affirmation of the happiness you have had.

The Sixth step

Increase the level of subtle energy within. What if your holiday Resort plunges into darkness, because of electricity failure? You have to access different sources of energy. Learn the techniques of increasing the level of energy within: Deep breathing, *Pranayama*, mantras (*Aum* or the Adi Mantras) or *Mudras* (there are more than thousand). Choose the technique your subtle body accepts easily, that gives you 'great' energy.

Will this Holiday resort within work? Well, try it. It has worked for many, why not for you?

> When you want something, the whole universe conspires in helping you to achieve it.
> **Paulo Coelho**